The Survivor

Lynne Schulz

Lulu Enterprises

THE SURVIVOR

© 2015 by National Twin Loss Support. All rights reserved.

First Published 2003, by Pleasant Word, a division of WinePress Publishing,

PO Box 428, Enumclaw, WA, 98022, USA.

First edition printed in the United States of America.

Second edition published 2014, Lulu Enterprises, 3101 Hillsborough Street, Raleigh, N.C, 27607, USA.

Second edition produced in Print-on-Demand and e-book formats

Ultimate design, content, and editorial accuracy of this work are the responsibilities of National Twin Loss Support, PO Box 3157, Salisbury East, South Australia, Australia.

No part of this publication may be reproduced, stored in a retrieval system, or transmitted in any form or by any means, electronic, mechanical, photocopying, recording or otherwise, without the prior permission of the copyright holders, except as provided by Australian and USA copyright law.

Unless otherwise noted, all Scriptures are taken from the Good News Bible, Australian Bicentennial Edition, Copyright © 1988.

Manuscript editor first edition: Jane Warland

Manuscript editor second edition: Les Dicker

Design Consultant second edition: Sean McPherson

Front cover photo 'Rhys' by Lynne Harford

Back cover photo 'Lynne' by Sean McPherson

ISBN: 978-1-326-17656-3

Content ID: 16117401

Dedication

Dedicated to Megan's Surviving Twin,

Rhys Antony Schulz.

"Sometimes half a picture is all I see

But I love you just the same;

For sometimes that picture which I see

Is the thing that keeps me sane."

(Your Mother)

Contents

Dedication	Page	3
Foreword	Page	7
Acknowledgments	Page	13
Preface	Page	17
Chapter 1 – Did I Say The Wrong Thing?	Page	27
Chapter 2 – A Mental Perspective	Page	35
Chapter 3 – A Mother's Perspective	Page	43
Chapter 4 – A Father's Perspective	Page	55
Chapter 5 – Common Survivor Behaviour	Page	67
Chapter 6 – Disabilities and other Concerns	Page	93
Chapter 7 – Effects on Higher Order Multiples	Page	107
Chapter 8 – Should I Tell the Truth?	Page	123
Chapter 9 – Memory Triggers	Page	133
Chapter 10 – Culture and Mystery	Page	153
Chapter 11 – The Future?	Page	167
References	Page	183
Further Reading	Page	187

Glossary	Page	189
Useful Organisations	Page	193
Appendix I –National Twin Loss Support	Page	197
Appendix II- Expert List	Page	205
Appendix III – Care Investigation	Page	209

Foreword

After the birth of our twin daughters over thirty years ago, I became very involved with our local multiple birth support organization. About two years later "a friend of a friend" was pregnant with twins and I spoke to her several times, offering tips, commiserating with her desire to be able to "sleep on her stomach" and sharing the joys of her impending birth. Only her story didn't have the same ending as mine. One of her daughters lived only a short while after birth. The couple was devastated. They lost their daughter, they lost a unique parenting experience, and they feared that they would lose their other daughter.

When I spoke to the grieving Mom, she was confused, dazed, angry and in despair. She said she was "afraid to love her surviving daughter because what if she died too?" She lost her baby, and it didn't seem that anyone else cared. As she explained, the doctor and nurses in attendance at the birth had focused on the live birth and "glossed over" the death of their baby. At the time, there was no encouragement to see a dead baby, hold, bathe or name them, let alone take any photos.

There was no literature to which I could refer her, nor research on loss in multiple births. Our local multiple birth support organization did not feel that they should remain members. Additionally, local grief counsellors did not know or recognize how to support them. Theirs was a loss without a name. They were re-victimized by uninformed others. I never heard from the mother again and to this day, I imagine the family as set adrift in a boat without paddles, as everyone watched from the shoreline, eyes cast downward.

Witnessing such experiences brought me to the step of trying to support and understand what these families suffer. Why was there not one single support system in our community which could or would actively support them? As they had one live birth and one death, why were they considered "different" from other bereaved parents? They still had lost a child and yet the simultaneity of life and death seemed to obliterate the opportunity for grieving in this situation. No doubt society puts a premium on life over death but a death that is not properly acknowledged and mourned can interfere greatly in our capacity to live. In this case, everyone, including the healthcare system, turned away from this couple's need to grieve at the same time they were welcoming their other baby into the world.

Families with survivors face a particularly difficult situation because they have a constant reminder in front of them of what should have been. They have had to deal with two extreme emotions at the same time; the joy of giving birth and the despair of loss of a baby or babies. They often suffer thoughtless and callous remarks from family and friends: "You never could have handled triplets. You've got two babies who need you - stop moping and get on with it!" – or; "Don't worry, it will fade and you'll find joy in the baby you have." Yet, truthfully, the identity of the baby who died is always a part of the parents' experience. It is inevitable that, as time passes, such parents will at least mentally compare their children: Would they both have had brown eyes? Would they have both been athletic, or musical, or good in math?

These sad families are forced to celebrate a birthday and a deathday, sometimes on the same day, year after year. Their grief journey is filled with challenges and comparisons to what should have been. In this regard, it is a loss without a remedy.

One child does not replace another, no matter how many you have. Each child is precious, no matter how short their stay with us. Each child leaves its mark within us and the fact that there may be survivors of a multiple birth doesn't make that mark any less indelible. In addition, the survivors are robbed of the special relationship and connection that womb-mates share.

Thankfully, much has changed. Books like *The Survivor* have been written to enlighten parents, grandparents, bereavement counsellors and the healthcare professionals who look after us better understand the conflicting feelings of life and loss together, and re-enforce that we, the bereaved parents, aren't crazy in the aftermath of these types of losses.

Because of better awareness put forth in books such as *The Survivor*, chapters have opened their doors a little wider to offer grieving families support. Multiple-birth bereavement support organizations have been developed, bereavement articles are more readily available covering many aspects of loss in multiple-birth, research is being conducted on the impact on survivors of the loss of their co-multiple and the many challenges bereaved families face are finally recognized.

My heartiest congratulations to Lynne Schulz (nee Harford), (Founder, National Twin Loss Support), in creating this important support tool for bereaved families' use and in sharing her and her son's story. *The Survivor* is essential support reading for parents, grandparents, healthcare workers, researchers and the bereavement counsellors who support them.

Lynda P. Haddon
Multiple Birth Educator
Multiple Birth: Prenatal Information & Bereavement Support
w.w.w.jumelle.ca

Acknowledgments

There are so many people who have made this book possible that it is difficult to know where to begin. My partner Sean has always supported my work and without his encouragement I would probably have never progressed very far with this 2nd edition update at all. My son Rhys was happy for me to write another book based on his, and his deceased twin sister Megan's life, and I thank him for allowing me to do this. I thank my sons Eric and Owen for their patience and understanding.

Jane Warland has been a wonderful support, as always. Especially with the first edition, Jane proved invaluable in her ability to access the professional and medical journals that I was unable to. She gladly assisted me, even though she was extremely busy with her own family and work. Jane has also undertaken important research into some of the reasons for infant loss. Dr Jane Warland PhD, has become a renown University Lecturer, widely respected for her work; often invited to medical conferences as a key note speaker.

I have been extremely fortunate to have 'crossed paths' with so many wonderful people. People such as Julie Bryant of OzMOST (Australia), Elizabeth Pector, (United States), and Lynda Haddon of the Multiple Birth Prenatal Education and Bereavement Support Group (Canada), were especially generous and supportive with their advice and research assistance.

Special thank you to the following mothers who participated in the National Twin Loss Support Survey of 2008-2010 relating to the quality and type of care of families after loss, whose responses can be found in Appendix III:

Joanne – Canada	Elizabeth – Canada
Jane – New Zealand	Kim – Australia
Jenny – Australia	Angela – Australia
Bindi – Australia	Anonymous – Australia
Annette – Australia	Linda – Australia
Narelle – Australia	Emily – United States
Sylvia – Australia	Sally – Australia

Rachell – New Zealand

Thanks must also go to the following parents, who kindly shared their stories in order for the world to be more aware of twin loss, and higher order multiple loss issues:

Nina Carlisle	Catie Olson
Leonie Harrison	Julie Ruiz
Tracy Louw	Rosemary Smart
Joanne Mathers	Elizabeth Pector
Jenny Stanley	Dearne O'Kane

Marcey Wilder

And most importantly, it wouldn't be right if I didn't acknowledge all the survivors and their siblings who allowed me to share their stories:

April and Erin (dec.) Carlisle

Matthew and Stephen (dec.) Harrison

Lisa and Amy (dec.) Louw

Matthew and Jessica (dec.) Mathers

Madeline Elise and Annelise (dec.) O'Kane

Jared and Bryan (dec.) Pector

Sam and Sarah (dec.) Olson

Frankie, Petey and Cecilia (dec.) Ruiz

Shannon Rublee, and siblings, Anna (dec.) and Neal (dec.)

Emily and Katie (dec.) Smart

Kate and Ben (dec.) Stanley

Noah, Gabreyella and Lyndsay (dec.) Wilder.

Preface

"You must be the change

you wish to see in the world."

(Mahatma Ghandi)

My first book, "The Diary" was an introduction to maternal loss and grief in a multiple pregnancy situation. It addressed the issues of how families were, and in some cases still are, treated by the medical profession, and society as a whole, when they lose one of their twins. Since I am the parent of a 'surviving twin', I tend to focus on that particular area.

However, families who experience the loss of precious babies from a triplet, quadruplet, or other higher order multiple pregnancies also experience similar treatment from family, friends, and other professionals. As my son is only recognised by the majority of society as a 'singleton' child, so other families have to endure recognition of their surviving triplets as 'twins', or their surviving quadruplet as a 'singleton', for example. It is another painful, often unexpected side of the grieving process, and is the constant daily reminder of what they have actually lost.

When I first began my work in the area of twin loss I was advised by 'experts' in both the publishing and medical fields, that this was such a small, insignificant area, and that there wouldn't be many people in a similar situation. I have been both amazed and shocked by the massive size of this particular region of infant loss, which still continues to receive very little public recognition, even more than twenty-four years after the death of my daughter Megan.

Loss in multiple pregnancies is a massive issue world wide, and continues to be exacerbated by the reliance upon fertility drugs and IVF programmes. There is no doubt that such treatments increase the risk of perinatal death of one or both twins and therefore I feel it is vital to make the medical profession aware of the broader consequences of some of their actions.

My journey through life, both as a bereaved parent and a volunteer bereavement counsellor, has been extremely varied and interesting. Although I have met so many wonderful people through what are initially, devastating circumstances, the resulting friendships seem to make these experiences all the more bearable....well, from my perspective anyway.

One of my closest friends, Jane Warland, has become a strong advocate of twin loss. Jane has experienced two singleton losses, (miscarriage and stillbirth), yet continues to 'push the barrow' so to speak, in the fight to get the subject of 'twin loss' more openly discussed within the medical professional arena. Her third book, "The Midwife and the Bereaved Family" is testimony to this, with a full chapter devoted to loss in a multiple pregnancy situation, and guidelines and suggestions for midwives to follow.

Now, I am definitely not denying that great progress has been made in how the medical profession handles infant loss overall. Modern society has made vast improvements from when babies were treated as disposable items, quite often removed with the garbage or hidden away in mass graves. It is marvellous how parents are now supported in spending as much time as possible with their dead babies, and the idea of 'memory creation', (i.e. creating tangible evidence such as footprints, poems, photos, etc.), is actively encouraged.

Sadly, most of these 'leaps and bounds' in the advancement of bereavement care mainly evolve around singleton loss, whilst the parents who experience equally devastating multiple loss are still told to be grateful for what they have, and then shut out from any further care and support. I am horrified to continually hear of situations within Australia for example, where major maternity hospitals label patient files of twin loss parents as 'singleton', simply to avoid confronting the 'too hard' basket.

One of the most devastating cases that I have ever heard of involved a situation where the body of a dead male twin, (born intact in the membrane), was literally plonked into a bucket, briefly shown to the shocked parents and then sent to different pathology units until someone was sensitive enough to act appropriately towards this baby.

I am sure that it wouldn't have happened with a singleton and the reason why he was treated so poorly was, he was a twin. He was considered an optional extra whose humanity wasn't valued because he had a living, breathing sister! Another unfortunate situation involved a woman who was handed her baby wrapped and taped in plastic, ready to take to the morgue.

Any pregnancy loss is a painful and tragic event. However, parents who suffer multiple pregnancy loss, live with their reminders on a daily basis as they look upon their cherished survivors and watch them grow.

> With the loss of a twin, however, the actual number of 'occasions' are increased exponentially witnessing growth

markers in the surviving twin ... the surviving twin is, ironically, the never-ending reminder of what could have been. [(Swanson-Kauffman, 1988), in Warland, J., 2000)].

Therefore in my view, even though I battle the opinions of those 'authorities' mentioned earlier, twin loss is still a neglected area that needs and deserves more public awareness and sensitivity than it is currently receiving. Hopefully, this second book, (which is aimed primarily at parents of surviving multiples), will continue to promote further education of this. It is hoped that this book may eventually become a useful resource for medical professionals and other carers of families who suffer multiple pregnancy loss because it will give them an insight into the lives and emotions of the families under their care.

During 2008-2010 I offered multiple birth loss families the opportunity of completing a survey to review the situation of multiple birth loss care by health care professionals, as well as investigate the levels of support provided by family and friends. Fifteen mothers from countries such as Australia, New Zealand, the USA and Canada took part, and the results were mixed, with some sharing that the support they had received after their loss/es was brilliant, whilst others confided that they had been treated poorly. The results of this investigation can be found in Appendix III.

As a further note in this book; when referring to lone twins, I personally prefer to use the term, 'survivor' because it instills in a person's mind a sense of positive strength. The term 'lone twin' is an apt term because it introduces the loneliness that many surviving twins state they feel.

Many people use the term, 'twinless twin' and although this too is a most suitable description of the same situation, I have chosen to use the term "survivor" throughout this book. Therefore the term, 'survivor' will feature more prominently than some of the other commonly used terminologies;

hopefully without offence to any twin loss organisation that may feel differently.

In this text I have utilized a number of experts. I believe that you should be aware of both who they are and their credentials, so I have created an 'Expert List' towards the end of this book in Appendix II, to refer to if you wish to know more about the expert whom I am quoting.

Don't Give Up Hope!

"Often multiple birth loss families give up on the hope of a bright future, particularly during the early years of the grieving process. However, the challenge that such families face, that makes multiple pregnancy loss so unique to singleton pregnancy loss, is that the families often have to cope with death and life together."

(Used with permission from the NTLS brochure 'Don't give up Hope!')

Chapter 1

DID I SAY THE WRONG THING?

"Understanding requires not just a moment of perception, but a continuous awareness, a continuous state of inquiry without conclusion."
(Bruce Lee).

Saying the 'wrong' thing, or simply just being caught with your foot literally jammed in your mouth, would have to be one of life's most dreaded moments. People should be encouraged to be honest in asking a bereaved person how they really feel and avoid clichéd comments. However, since we are all only human, I feel confident in saying that I am sure that at one stage in our lives, at least, we have probably said something that we have later regretted.

The problem regarding bereavement care, and especially twin loss, is that the people who make the hurtful comments, genuinely don't realise that they have said anything 'wrong'. I have been in the situation where, shortly after I came home from the hospital with my surviving twin Rhys, the two people that I was involved in conversation with began joking about the work of having two babies. One of them was a singleton mother and looked at me, laughing and stated, "Thank goodness we don't have two babies, hey Lynne!" To which I coldly replied, "I did have two babies" turned my back, walked away, and haven't spoken to her since.

Over the years, I have found that a bit of tact, diplomacy and a genuine apology can go a long way in fixing an accidental verbal 'oops'. For the trauma of loss in a multiple pregnancy runs deep and never ends – it only blurs a bit around the edges with time.

Although there is no particular 'right' word to say when anyone dies, there are some definite phrases of which we could steer well clear. This especially holds true in the case of multiple pregnancy loss, where it is generally taken for granted by societal ignorance, that because there is still a living baby, (or babies in some cases), everything is alright. Basically, it is like being compared to a female dog having a litter of pups, with the main concern being that the bulk of the litter is safe, healthy and happy. As I have replied over the years, "I am not canine, and I did not give birth to a litter of pups!"

I shouldn't have to remind the medical profession, (i.e. doctors and midwives), that what they say has a major impact on their patients. However, some medical professionals seem to have forgotten this basic rule of common sense and human sensitivity. Surely professional people could think of other terms in which to describe a deceased infant apart from 'a piece of meat', (as in my own situation), or 'like a pancake'. These ignorant and foolish references to food items are completely unnecessary, and only further exacerbate the emotional scarring that the parents may have already endured.

Jane Warland shares some of those awful cliché phrases that people tend to mention in times of grief, and that most of us have probably heard at one time or another during our own losses. It is hoped that after reading this chapter, comments such as these may be avoided in the future by medical professionals, carers, counsellors, and of course, ourselves:

- 'At least you have the other twin'
- 'You can always have another baby'
- 'It was God's will'
- 'If you had to lose him, at least it happened now instead of after you had really gotten attached to him'
- 'The one you have keeps you up all night and demands all of your attention, how would you have managed having two?' (Warland, J., Jul. 2000)

People just don't realise how powerful words are. They can build people up and make them feel wonderful and understood. They can tear people apart and drag them down to absolute desperation and despair.

Society enjoys using common phrases such as 'at least'. Personally, I feel that we could eliminate this one altogether unless referring to mathematics or talking about the size of an object. Apart from that, this phrase sends out such a negative message.

Try this little substitution trick that I invented during my early grieving years. Whenever you are about to say, "at least", make an abrupt mental halt, and replace it with, "it's good". For example, "at least you still have a baby" could be turned completely around into "it's good you still have a baby". It works every time. I often challenge people that I speak to, to try it. It becomes positively habit-forming.

Modern society in particular, has a horrible habit of referring to infants who have died as 'replaceable commodities', like purchasing a new packet of cereal from the supermarket. Not all couples have an easy time in falling pregnant. It is devastating to see couples who have endured IVF programmes for years, experience the cruelty of infant loss, sometimes repeatedly. So in fact, to tell someone that they can easily replace their dead baby is an extremely hurtful and ignorant comment to make. Afterall, would you tell someone whose mother had died to simply go out and get another one?

Relying on the surviving twin to make the pain go away just doesn't work. We ponder questions such as,

> Why can't our live, healthy child take all this pain away? Why can't we focus on what we have; instead of the things we have lost? (Schulz, L., Dec. 1998).

We blame God for everything that goes wrong in the world, when in fact we should be asking him to love us all the more. We are, at the end of the day, only human beings that thrive on emotion. We need to grieve for the loved ones we have lost and it shouldn't matter when and how those loved ones were born, how long they lived; or when they died.

Grieving is hard work. It is mentally and physically draining. When you consider that the grieving process can take years to struggle through, no wonder people end up so exhausted. Just put yourself in the shoes of a mother with a surviving twin. She has to cope with the twenty-four hour demands of a new infant. She also has to cope with the energy draining effects of her grief. Now, imagine the hurtful comments about not being able to cope. Just doesn't seem fair, does it?

Maternal bonding can take place during very early stages of pregnancy. Most women who experience pregnancy will tell you that they remember all the little movements and kicks inside the womb. They know when their unborn babies are asleep or awake. They cherish the ultrasound photos from their medical checkups and notice every minute change that occurs to their bodies, both internally and externally. They talk, sing, read stories and play music to their unborn babies. If mothers only formed attachments to their babies after birth, there wouldn't be the need for a lot of the prenatal bereavement care organisations in the world today.

Chapter 2

A MENTAL PERSPECTIVE

"It is not the end of the physical body

that should worry us.

Rather, our concern must be to live while we're alive".

(Elizabeth Kubler-Ross)

Family relationships on the whole can be extremely complex and intertwined. This can make the family unit a difficult subject to study and fully comprehend at the best of times, let alone during a crisis such as a death. Throw in the issues faced in the difficulties of twin loss and you find yourself almost walking amongst an invisible minefield.

Joan Woodward, states that during her studies of twin loss, the clearest finding ... was that the loss of a twin is a very profound one. (Woodward, J., 1999).
She found that losses occurring before six years of age seemed to have the most significant effect on the survivors.

This can perhaps be attributed to the fact that young babies have no real understanding of death as such, and are therefore not really able to comprehend their emotions. There is also the primary socialisation process involving a person's 'family of orientation', i.e. the family into which we are born. Family contact, particularly parental influences are daily distractions emanating from involvement in family life. Such distractions may cause emotions associated with early sibling loss to become hidden, and not revealed until later years. As the socialisation process moves into the secondary phase evolving around schooling and education, these bottled up emotions may rise to the surface and become more prominent in behavioural patterns.

Woodward uses the 'Attachment Theory' by John Bowlby as a basis for explaining some of the early relationships established by surviving twins and their immediate family members. Attachment Theory examines the way in which human beings make their strong bonds of affection within the family unit. Bowlby's own study of maternal bonding caused him to conclude that the ability to create bonds is due to humans being determined by *instinctive behaviours*, just as all other animals are, in order to ensure their survival. (Woodward, J., 1999).

This theme is again used to expand on the notion that proper Attachment lies at the heart of the development of a 'sense of self'. (Woodward, J, 1999).

This is Woodward's terminology for the journey to self-discovery, the establishing of self-esteem and finding out who you really are.

> Attachment Theory provides the biological evidence of our need as humans to form Attachments. ... both Attachments and the loss of them, or threat of loss, at any time of life, affect our state of mental health. (Woodward, J., 1999).

The fact that twins may find it more difficult than singletons to establish a strong sense of their own unique identities, is probably due to the concept of being a 'pair'. Together they form a whole unit, therefore when one twin dies, the bond is broken and the unit becomes incomplete. The twin unit itself possesses all the characteristics that are usually possessed by a singleton child and when one twin is left alone due to death, for example, the whole picture seems to appear slightly out of balance. That is why I quite often use the phrase 'seeing half a picture' when I speak of my son Rhys. It is not a critical term, just a simple observation.

Care needs to be taken when speaking about personal theories and observations because they can often be misconstrued as irrelevant or ridiculous thoughts, especially by some members of the medical profession. But learning to listen to what people have to say is a valuable tool in bereavement care, as well as in general life.

Linda G. Leonard also acknowledges some of the valid points discussed by people such as Woodward, Piontelli and Pector as she addresses important areas of early twin loss including miscarriage and vanishing twin syndrome;

> … what a twin fetus might miss is not a complete person but the stimulation arising from and the comfort provided by the co-twin. It is unknown if the stimulation between the

pair becomes "forever embedded in the subconscious of the surviving twin". ... There are anecdotal accounts from various therapists of emotionally aggrieved survivors when a twin miscarries, such as occurs in "vanishing twin syndrome." ... Woodward conducted an extensive study of lone twins and discovered that the distress felt by the twin whose co-twin died at or around birth may occur even when the survivor is unaware of being a twin.

Some multiple-birth survivors, especially those who lose a monozygotic or dizygotic multiple of the same gender, report a pervasive feeling that something is missing or has been lost, endlessly searching for an attachment that cannot be found, intense and constant loneliness, and guilt. ... Whether or not the fetus has a psychic memory is controversial. (Leonard, L. G., Oct. 2001).

It is important for bereaved parents themselves to remember, (especially during the early days of their grief), that they are not thinking clearly. Chemical imbalances within the human body through the initial shock stay within the body for months.

They can result in memory loss, vagueness, loss of appetite, lack of concentration and mood swings'. (Schulz, L., Dec. 1998).

Useful recovery aids such as keeping a diary, writing poetry, or taking notes, are definitely valuable tools, which could eventually be utilized in assisting other bereaved parents. Therefore, support groups that have been established by bereaved mothers can provide an important and vital avenue through which to form new friendships and to talk about personal experiences in a supportive and non-threatening environment.

Elizabeth Pector, concludes this chapter perfectly:

> We may never know whether medical problems or unusual behaviours in a surviving multiple are related to the child's inborn genetic traits, pregnancy or birth complications, physical or psychological trauma from the loss, parenting

style, or family grief responses. Psychological relationships between intact sets of multiple children have not been studied as thoroughly as one might expect. Psychologists' opinions vary on the impact of womb experiences on children and adults. Many are skeptical about the significance of losing a wombmate shortly after birth. On the other hand, anecdotes and studies verify the importance of these losses for survivors and their families. Each family needs to draw their own careful conclusions after considering the information that applies to their particular circumstances. (Pector, E. A., Jan. 2001).

Chapter 3

A MOTHER'S PERSPECTIVE

"It is your own face that you see reflected in the water and it is your own self that you see in your heart".

(Proverbs 27 v19)

Mothers are in the unique and special position of being able to bond with their unborn babies during pregnancy. This physical and emotional connection is considered by some as unconsciously occurring almost from the moment of conception. We make plans for our unborn children, create marvellous nurseries, and prepare our homes to welcome our new arrivals. The phrase 'feathering the nest' is thus commonly associated with pregnant women who are preparing their households in readiness for their anticipated new arrivals.

Another interesting part of pregnancy is 'intuition'. A woman's intuition, (or that little voice inside), which was once scoffed at by medical professionals, is now being treated with more dignity and seriousness. It is because of the bond between the mother and child, or children in the case of a multiple pregnancy, that a woman has the distinct advantage of knowing when something is not quite right. In many cases of infant loss, women who felt that there was something wrong during their pregnancies, were more often than not, correct.

One mother of a surviving twin believed that she knew that one of her babies would die.

> Then I rang my Mum and sobbed out the words "one of my babies is dead!" She came to the surgery immediately and all of a sudden I remembered a dream I'd had early that morning that one of my babies would die. I woke, dismissed the dream and had completely forgotten about it ... but then when I remembered, I went into shock! (Bryant, J., 2002).

Even though societal changes have openly accepted that many fathers choose to stay at home to look after their young children, it is still mostly the women who fulfill this role. Women therefore have more time than men to observe the small, daily changes that occur during those early years of childhood. We are the ones who hand out the discipline, carry out the first aid, wipe the runny noses and amongst numerous other things, provide the emotional comfort to our children.

It should be noted that even after a successful pregnancy, some mothers grieve. I personally felt a loss in losing that close constant physical attachment when my babies were bundled up inside my womb.

Although it was wonderful to be able to see my toes again and stand closer to the sink when washing the dishes, there was a strange feeling that something had been taken away. I no longer had sole responsibility of carrying my children. Things had somehow changed.

I cherished the moments when I could lay on the bed or lounge and feel my unborn children kicking inside my womb. It was a special relationship that only another mother could truly understand. I always felt that whilst my babies were still inside me, I could keep them safe and protected from the rest of the world. However, any loss that occurs during pregnancy will definitely rob a woman of that naive and blissful state-of-mind.

When something goes wrong in a pregnancy a mother can feel that she has failed her unborn child or children in a major way. She may feel she has failed in providing the safe protected haven that should have been there. She can think that she has lost control of what her body does and this can cause endless emotional pain and frustration.

Losses that occur in a multiple pregnancy are even more traumatic for the mother. In my own situation of twin loss,

> I found it difficult to cope with the fact that my body was slowly destroying one of the most precious gifts that I had ever received. And I could do absolutely nothing about it! My body then sent out conflicting signals saying "stop!". It could not carry out shut-down procedures because there was still life inside. I lived too far away from the hospital for the specialist to keep an eye on me, so I had to stay in the hospital. Each day I was watched and monitored to ensure that I, and the surviving baby, were still alright. (Schulz, L., Dec. 1998).

It is usually the mother who creates the tangible reminders that her child, or children even existed, especially in situations of miscarriage where there is very little if any, physical evidence that the woman was even pregnant at all. The Chapter, Memory Triggers looks further into the issues of memory creation.

Apart from finding solace in our grief, and a purpose to it all, creating physical reminders of our deceased children assists in a positive way in helping to introduce them to the rest of the world. It is difficult for friends and relatives to understand our situation when they haven't had an actual baby to hold and look at. Our surviving twins and other higher order multiples, as stated throughout this book, become to us, the most tangible evidence of all – the constant daily reminder of what we have actually lost.

It is indeed a great shock to some, but usually exciting, for most mothers to be told by the doctor that they are going to have twins, triplets, quadruplets, etc.

The loss of one or even all babies thus becomes even more traumatic. One mother of two surviving triplets shared her feelings after finding out that she was carrying three babies.

> Before we knew the sexes of the babies, I wanted them to be two boys and a girl, so when we found out that this was the case, I couldn't have been happier! I pictured two boys protecting their sister. Growing up together and being that close to a sibling that is the opposite sex gives you a better understanding of them ... I also felt, (during my pregnancy), that if I wanted to I could be done having kids since I had all I wanted. (Ruiz, J., email).

As previously mentioned; mothers plan. We imagine what our babies look like inside the womb and what colour their eyes and hair will be. We think about how they shall be dressed, which toys they will play with, and even enroll them in pre-school and primary school. When this personal moment of joy is shattered a woman may feel robbed of her chance to be a mother to a multiple birth family. She may have looked forward to being able to have all her children in one pregnancy, never to have to face the thought of ever being pregnant again.

It can be extremely stressful when a mother who has spent months enduring an uncomfortable multiple pregnancy, finally gives birth, only to have to watch one or more babies struggle in isolettes and on life support systems. One mother whose triplet daughter died almost two weeks after birth shared the following:

> To watch your baby fight a deadly battle for ten days is torture. I will say this, it does "help" to prepare you. You eventually start asking God to just save the child in whatever way He sees fit. You stop asking to keep the child here on Earth because you realise that it may be a selfish request; because of what she is going through. I was,

thankfully, able to hold her for her last twenty minutes of life. She began with me, and ended with me. (Ruiz, J., email).

Many bereaved mothers will state that they would have rather had their children for a short time, than never to have had them at all. In my own situation, I often sat and wondered what life would have been like without my daughter Megan. Would it have made me a better person? Would I have been any happier?

Although it would have been nice to not have endured the devastation of watching my child's life ebb away as her placenta slowly died, I feel that what she gave me in return more than made up for any pain that I initially felt. Megan made me a more compassionate and understanding person. I have become more patient and sensitive to other twin loss mothers, and I have learnt how to appreciate life and live it to its fullest potential.

I feel her presence, even now after all these years. Is it just a wishful thought? Sometimes I turn around suddenly expecting to see someone standing behind me, but when I turn around, there is no one there. Sometimes I feel that I am being watched by unseen eyes, but I am sitting in an empty room. Do our deceased children stay with us? Do they in turn watch over and protect us, hopefully from some of the horrors of the real world? I would like to think so. I will leave that thought with you ...

The importance of a positive approach.

"The support from friends and family received by any grieving family is paramount to a successful and eventual, positive recovery. Therefore, if those around us can recognise and acknowledge multiple birth loss in a positive way, and not dismiss it as a 'strange idea from a mother who can't accept what life has thrown at her', then the surviving multiple birth child will grow up in a more positive psychological frame of mind."

(Used with permission from the NTLS brochure 'Don't give up Hope!')

Chapter 4

A FATHER'S PERSPECTIVE

"Courage is resistance to fear, mastery of fear –

not absence of fear".

(Mark Twain)

This chapter differs to the mother's perspective chapter because whether we like to acknowledge it or not, men are different to women, and always will be. Although I gave both the mothers and fathers the same opportunity to share their thoughts regarding behavioural observations regarding their survivors with me, I found that the fathers were reluctant. I therefore looked upon this situation, not as a defeat, but as a chance to investigate why fathers prefer not to write, and in doing so made reference to one dad in particular who lost a singleton child, but after much encouragement from his wife, finally found the courage to put pen to paper.

==Father's are often the forgotten ones during infant loss.== Everybody, from the medical staff to the grandparents tends to forget that it took two people to initially create the baby, and that males have emotions as well, albeit different ones. We, as females, must remember that the males are just as lost and lonely, and perhaps just as frightened about the whole deal', (Schulz, L., Dec. 1998), as we are. So, when it comes to speaking about experiences regarding infant loss, and twin loss issues, men are usually the last ones to be considered as having an opinion on the subject.

Many women that I have counselled over the years make the same complaint, "He just doesn't care!" Men have difficulty in understanding the situation, in expressing their needs. They have had to endure the event of pregnancy, from a distance because they are not the ones who carried the baby/ies inside their bodies, and are not the ones who had the unique opportunity of bonding early with the unborn child in the same way as we had.

Aside from the obvious biological differences men also have different emotional needs that are almost always forgotten during any form of emotional crisis. Many people in our society still seem extremely shocked to hear that men have emotional needs in the first place! No matter how modern our males appear to be, the echoes of past generational stereotyping keeps raising its head to totally confuse the situation.

> When a person is unable to hold all their emotions in any longer, they cry ... For women, our society seems to find crying quite acceptable, but for men, it is frowned upon. We need to be very understanding and very gentle with the person at this point, whether male or female. (Schulz, L., Dec. 1998).

==Men are expected to be strong, and support the family, and deal with both his own and his wife's emotions==. (Warland, J., 1996). ==They thus tend to involve themselves more in their work, in a desperate act to avoid both grieving and to be publicly seen as showing a moment's weakness==. It creates confusion and tension within a relationship, and can sadly, result in its eventual breakdown.

As I remind those women to whom I speak, it is vital to keep the lines of communication open. Once those lines close, the relationship is doomed. If you can manage to keep talking and listening to your partner, and telling him that you really want to understand how he is feeling too, then there is a good chance that the relationship will evolve into a more caring, loving and stable one. However, having said that, it is important to note that a relationship that was unstable in the first instance, will not necessarily be saved because a tragedy has occurred.

Women are more fortunate than men in times of emotional stress because we usually can sit ourselves at the kitchen table with a friend and a cuppa, and talk about almost any subject that pops into our heads. Females can spend hours talking about the most basic things in life. Most men sit and shake their heads in amazement at this skill, unable to comprehend how the female tongue doesn't wear out from overuse, or wonder why our vocal cords don't overheat from sheer exhaustion. Most men don't realise how important this kind of emotional therapy is to a woman.

Likewise, most men don't feel comfortable sitting around the kitchen table talking for hours. I live in rural South Australia and have observed that men, particularly farmers, find it difficult to understand why people can sit around and waste precious time when there are numerous tasks awaiting attention. Often I will advise women that men like to talk when they're doing something that is important to them, like fixing the car, or mending fences in a paddock. I am well aware of how grossly stereo-typed my ideas appear, but they tend to be very true, particularly in rural regions where men think they have to be tough and strong, like their fathers and grandfathers before them.

Guys also seem to enjoy sitting with a mate watching sports such as football and cricket. In this type of situation, I often suggest that a beer and pizza evening can work wonders when trying to encourage a bereaved father to open up and tell somebody how he is really feeling. Men don't feel comfortable crying in front of anyone, most of all a woman.

However, if they can find an environment in which they can be honest with themselves, then they too will discover some of that emotional healing that we females find around the common kitchen table.

Another point of interest that I have discovered through my work as a bereavement counsellor, is that most males honestly don't realise that they have the capabilities to be emotionally open with each other in the first place. Often they have to be told quite bluntly that they can actually fulfill this most basic task in life that millions of women take for granted each day.

When considering the issue of infant death, once men have gone through the initial shock of discovering that they can be emotionally open with another person, it is usually a good time to encourage both parents to see if they can be honest with each other. A quiet moment together such as walking through a garden, watching a sunset, or strolling along a beach, establishes a positive and undistracted environment in which communication can occur. If the couple is able to talk to each other, and really listen to how the other feels, then these renewed lines of communication have generally opened up enough to allow the relationship to be strengthened.

Although Jane Warland's husband Mike suffered a singleton loss, his personal experience can be just as useful to fathers who suffer multiple pregnancy loss. Many of his emotions were similar to his wife's. Just like Jane, Mike realised that he too had to work through new and alarming emotional changes, both within himself as well as within his relationship with her.

> The loss of Emma caused many significant changes to my relationship with Jane. A stubborn accountant and an emotional midwife do not have a lot to discuss about their work which the other can understand. Prior to this event, it was quite common for me to resolve an argument, by walking out the back door to do some work in the garden until we both cooled down. I believed that this was the best solution in cases where there had to be a winner or the

> argument could only get worse. Hence it has been considerable change for us to actually sit down and discuss our feelings especially as I was very reluctant about sharing my own feelings. (Warland, J., 1996)

Jane and Mike discovered that the loss of our children can at times strengthen our marriages because we know that we have to help each other through the crisis. Both partners also realise that there is someone with them who understands what it is like to lose a precious and much-loved baby, becoming an emotional lifeline for each other in an environment where many of those them do not fully understand what the couple are experiencing. Mike summed up his own personal situation extremely well:

> I honestly believe that in our case the loss of Emma has saved our marriage, through having to rely strongly on each other to get through our crisis. It has also had a strengthening effect on our children, who have been included in many of our decisions.

It would have been very easy to get immersed in my work, then come home to sit in front of the television, and close-up my emotions. However, through opening up I have learned of many inner strengths in myself, but especially in my wife and children.

The most important part of our family now, in addition to the improved communication, is the intuitive understanding of the emotional roller coaster we face. (Warland, J., 1996).

Mike was very conscious of being regarded as a perfect example of what to do, and made the following comments to hopefully deter others from regarding him as a hero:

> Before the ladies put me on a pedestal, and I get hung by the males who are shown this chapter and asked "Why can't you understand how I feel, like this man can?", I must answer the question. **How can I understand how my wife feels?** The answer to this question is simple ... I can't! (Warland, J., 1996).

I want to leave the fathers with one final thought in this chapter. Don't be frightened to listen to that little voice inside you. And yes, you do actually have a little voice inside you that you should occasionally be listening to! Don't forget to take a moment every now and again to be still, and quiet and reflect upon life's issues. And most importantly, don't forget to involve yourself in the life of your surviving twin, or higher order multiples because they need both their parents to guide, love and support them.

> **Acknowledge your child's status.**
>
> "By acknowledging your surviving multiple birth child's status, i.e. twin, triplet, etc., you help them to grow up feeling comfortable in sharing their emotions, and all family members learn how to celebrate their special status in life in a positive way."
>
> *(Used with permission from the NTLS brochure 'Don't give up Hope!')*

Chapter 5

COMMON SURVIVOR BEHAVIOUR

"Do yourself a favour and learn all you can;

then remember what you learn

and you will prosper".

(Proverbs 19 v8)

This chapter is a collection of observations about surviving twins from a mother's viewpoint. It is up to each individual reader to decide whether too much has been assumed about the connection of surviving twins and the bonding they once shared with their deceased siblings, or whether what is shared is special and unique. I personally prefer the latter.

Imaginary friends.

Although it is common for young children to have an imaginary friend, some parents of surviving twins view this behaviour as an unconscious attempt to fill the void left by the twin who has died. A survivor should therefore not be of any great concern to the parent if they do display some of these behaviours.

Rhys' Story

An imaginary friend named, "Little Boy" (LB), resided in our household for the first two years until our next son Eric was born. LB was probably a minor source of amusement rather than a great concern. LB would generally be punished when Rhys was punished, and told off for being naughty when Rhys was told off.

Occasionally LB would come for rides in the family car, but I don't really recall him sitting with us at the dinner table. It was interesting to note that none of our other children had imaginary friends. LB would only appear when Rhys was on his own, not when other children were visiting our house, and although LB joined us in the family car, he never ventured out anywhere else except the car and our house.

Unexpected behaviours.

Occasionally all children will have some unexpected emotional outburst, such as a temper tantrum. More often than not a tantrum causes annoyance and embarrassment to a parent, especially if it occurs in public. However, the following story depicts an emotional outburst that was quite upsetting for me because of the link between the surviving twin and the deceased sibling.

Rhys' Story

One evening at age 5, Rhys suddenly became extremely upset and began screaming, "Why am I alive? Why didn't I die and my sister Megan live? I want to die too!" This was quite disturbing to witness, but after many consoling hugs and reassuring words, he calmed down. It was the only episode of its type to ever occur and it only ever happened the once – thankfully.

Selected friendships.

It has been noted by experts that surviving twins can have difficulty in forming long-term friendships. They may take a long time to establish a friendship with a particular child of the same age, and when that friendship link is broken, perhaps due to changing schools as in Rhys' case, the surviving twin has much trouble in re-establishing the same level of trust and friendship with another child.

It may even take years to mend the bond that has been broken. Another interesting point in Rhys' case was the fact that his strongest friendships appear to emulate part of the relationship that he may have had with his deceased twin sister, Megan as the bond appears to be formed with girls who have been the same age as she would have been.

Rhys' story

Rhys' strongest friendships have been with females his own age, but only three of them over a period of 12 years. At age 7, his special friend at the time just happened to be a twin herself and at times she and Rhys seemed to get along better than she did with her own twin sister.

Matthew's story

> *I have also noticed that people have to form the relationship with Matthew rather than the other way around. He needs acceptance and people to take an interest in him before he bonds with them. There has only been two people in Matt's life, (apart from relatives), that have formed strong bonds with Matt. He does not have trouble forming friends at school and gets invited to events such as birthdays etc., with his friends but the bonds with adults are the difficulty. (Harrison, L., email).*

Withdrawal into own world

Sometimes parents may notice that their surviving twins, or higher order multiples, (particularly if a sole survivor), 'disappear' into their own little world within their own minds. They appear to mentally withdraw from the room even when they might be right in the middle of a conversation and don't 'reappear' until a few moments later. Although this form of behaviour can be noted on thousands of occasions with singletons, it somehow seems a bit more startling when a survivor is involved. It also seems to annoy or concern the other family members much more than the surviving twin who experiences this behaviour, because they generally don't realise that they do it. This happened on frequent intervals in our own family with Rhys.

Rhys' story

Every now and again, particularly at the meal table when everyone was sitting having a meal, Rhys would mentally 'disappear' into his own little world. He would do this right in the middle of a conversation, which was extremely annoying for all of the family – except of course, for Rhys. It used to happen quite a lot when he was a young child, but it has decreased dramatically over the years. Our family refers to this as Rhys going off into "Rhys-land".

The most interesting thing to observe about this behaviour, was that it was never emulated by our other children, who were singleton boys, both born two and four years after Rhys.

In our family it is a behaviour uniquely belonging to Rhys, and Rhys alone. And although we just accept it as part of Rhys' twinship, it still annoys the heck out of us!

Fascination with images.

A number of parents have mentioned how their surviving twins are absolutely fascinated with images, such as their own reflection in a mirror, or their own shadows. It should be remembered that this is not a behaviour solely associated with surviving twins, and fascination with images is considered a normal part of a child's growing curiosity with life.

Thomas' Story

... it's interesting that you make mention of a fascination with images – Thomas loves mirrors and our tinted windows and will spend ages playing peek-a-boo with himself and he is just absolutely fascinated by this. I did wonder if this might be a 'twin thing'. He also found an old doll of mine and has a really strong association with 'Leah'. Sometimes he won't sleep unless he can see her and

he likes to share his milk with her and give her lots of cuddles. And again, I wondered if this was a 'twin thing'. (Bryant. J., email).

Jared's Story

Jared definitely had the fascination with reflections. He looks at his reflection in a window rather than looking through the window to see outside. Trying to get him to 'do his business" in the bathroom was an ordeal when he was about 3 years old.

He'd look at himself in the chrome fixtures, in the glossy pane in the bathroom stall, even in the toilet water! It would be nearly impossible to pry him away from mirrors in the clothing section of department stores. He still pays more attention than most children to his image in windows, the glossy paint of cars, etc. but this has declined significantly now that he is 6 years old. (Pector, E., email).

Unexplained experiences.

Sometimes things occur in life for which there is no apparent explanation. Humans have always been curious about the supernatural and some of the following stories are certainly something to think about.

Thomas' story.

I don't think the bond of twins can be under-estimated. John & I were sitting one day talking about Megan. Thomas was just a few days old & sound asleep in my arms but every time we said Megan's name his eyes would open & then he'd go back to his deep sleep again. And on Christmas Eve, when Thomas was 7 mths old, we had John's family visiting for Christmas dinner. While everyone was downstairs giving their dinner some time to digest, I took Thomas upstairs for his bath & bedtime.

As I didn't want everyone to hear me settling Thomas down, I turned his room monitor off at the power point. I was giving him his bath & suddenly we heard a tiny little child's voice calling through his room monitor, "Thomas, Thomas!" There is no logical explanation for this because that is the monitor which transmits the sounds downstairs & yet it was receiving sound and like I say, I had the power turned off. When Thomas was settled in his bed for the night I went downstairs & John asked, "Who was that calling for Thomas?" Everyone heard the voice. In my heart of hearts I know it was our Megan, though most people think I'm crazy for daring to believe that.

Something happened just the other day which reminded me of a few other inexplicable happenings in our household ... Thomas has a musical turtle and when you push the dome down it will play one of three tunes. The music won't play if the turtle is just lying on its back, the dome is designed so that when you push it down the music will play and a dice will roll around. Anyway, the other day I was giving Thomas his brekky and the turtle started to play all by itself. And when the first song finished it played the next one, and the next one ...

This has also happened with Thomas' other musical toy – a duck which, when you press its wing down, will play the alphabet song. (Again, it won't play if it is lying wing-side down, you have to apply a bit of pressure to get it to work).

And a few months ago Thomas and I were downstairs and we could hear the duck playing the alphabet song through his room monitor. It got to the end of the song and then played again. Curiosity got the better of me and I went upstairs and everything was just as we had left it. What am I to think of this? On another occasion Thomas was in the family room playing and I was at the kitchen sink and I felt a tug at my clothing, but when I looked down nobody was there.

People could so easily write these things off as delusional or wishful thinking, but too many things have happened for it to be just coincidence. I don't know if these are common happenings with people who have a strong connection with their deceased loved one, but I can't help but think that we

> *have a little visitor in our midst. It reassures me that Megan really isn't very far away at all. (Bryant, J., email)*

Interesting behaviour patterns.

Some of the behavioural patterns displayed by surviving twins, especially those of a particularly young age, appear extremely interesting. The survivor may behave in an angry and inconsolable manner, possibly due to the fact that they simply, miss their deceased twin. The twin unit is no longer a whole, and I truly believe that we will never fully understand the complex relationship that belongs solely to the world of twins. The next few stories share just a few of these types of behaviours.

Mitchell's Story

> *When he, (Mitchell), was first born, he was a very angry baby. They, (the hospital), had to basically tie him up or he would pull all his tubes out. ... the only time he really settled was when they put a little stuffed bunny in with him. I always noticed during our ultrasounds that he and Antony*

would move closer together while being monitored. It stuck in my mind how significant it was that they would both move to the side of their sac closest to the other. ...

We have a photo of Antony next to our bed and over the last few weeks, Mitchell keeps going over to it and smiles at him and then kisses him. He shows no interest in the photos of the other boys, or even himself. When he was small, he would look up to the corner of the room and smile for no apparent reason. He still will point to the ceiling and smile. He also loves to look at lights and when he was really little would smile at them. I can't really work it out as in every other way he is just like the other three.
(Sciacca. V., email).

Madeline's Story

Annelise's membranes ruptured at 22 weeks. She lived for 6 hours after her birth and these were the most bittersweet hours of my life. ... while we were there saying goodbye to her, Madeline was so unsettled. She cried consistently for the next few hours, as though she knew that her sister was leaving us. Annelise died at 8pm that night, Madeline seemed to settle not long after that.

...The next thing that comes to mind ... happened a year ago – 6th August 2001. My birthday. I had Madeline on my bed and she was 6 months corrected age, so still quite small. I was thanking her for being here with me to celebrate my birthday and I said to her "I'm sure your sister would have been here with us if things could have been different. Who knows? She's probably right here in this room with us." Madeline smiled at me and began talking to me like she was telling me something.

I hold this memory in my heart and I remember looking around the room for some kind of sign that she was there. Funny though, now I know I don't need signs, Madeline will be able to tell me.

...I had never been to the cemetery by myself until this year when I just woke up one morning and decided that Maddy and I would go. I was ready to do this. The date was 20th

April 2002. I was arranging the flowers that I had bought, Madeline was walking around close by. She toddled over to Annelise's grave and knelt down over the top of her teddy bear plaque and patted the teddy bear. She then stood up, turned and sat in my lap (by this stage I was weeping) and then waved to her sister's plaque. I was a mess. If ever I had doubted the fact that she was aware of her sister, I know now that she is with her everywhere and Madeline knows who we are visiting at the cemetery. This I am sure of.

We just celebrated the girls' 2nd birthdays yesterday and the anniversary of Annelise's death. ... Last year we named a star through the International Star Registry in memory of Annelise – Our Angel in Heaven. So, this year for her we decided to have the star certificate framed along with the clay hand and footprints that we took the night that she died.

The day that we took the above mentioned items to the framers Madeline was misbehaving quite badly. We were in someone else's home and I was unsure of what it was that she wanted. She became quite interested in Annelise's plaque and was trying with all of her might to get her hands on it, and when it was removed from her reach, the tears and tantrum grew worse. I said to Madeline, (all of 23 months old), "What is it? Do you want to touch this? OK, come over and touch it – it's the one and only time that you will get the chance." Well, the tantrum stopped. She walked over to me, bent down to the floor (where ... the plaque was), and kissed it. This had me in tears. ...

Two days before the girls' birthdays, the frame was delivered to our house, finally finished and looking just as I had imagined – beautiful. I was struggling with the frame to get it in the front door safely, I was holding the glass pressed to me and as I did this Madeline walked into the room, stopped in her tracks, pointed to the frame, (which she could only see the back of), and says, "Oh, Baby!". I just broke down in tears and asked her, "How do you know?. There was absolutely nothing to indicate the

contents of the frame. It's as if she knew that a part of Annelise was home again ...
(O'Kane. D., email).

Sam's Story

About Sam, he is physically very different from the other children. He has very dark hair and the only one of our four with dark brown eyes. He is also physically so beautiful and very small for his age, although he was our second biggest baby.

The thing that really astounds me is his intimate knowledge of death and life. He is fearful of everything, yet tries so desperately hard to be brave and strong. We mostly have children who jump into everything, but Sam is always at the edges.
(Olson, C., email)

Matthew's story.

The other significant thing with Matt is that from the time he could lift his head as a very small baby he would bang his head on his pillow while he was sleeping. The Paediatrician told me not to be concerned, that it was a 'comfort thing', like sucking his thumb. At 16 years old now he is still doing it, ...I don't really know if he feels different so much as if he wonders why he is here and his brothers are not.

When talking about his brothers I tell him I am so thankful that he stayed with us, as he was quite sick after he was born and that it is him who has lessened my grief by being here. It is important that he does not feel guilty about his surviving and that he does not blame himself and that he knows I do not blame him. He tends to need a lot of reassurance and encouragement with what he does, ... it is hard to distinguish what is his 'own' personality and what is the result of his twinlessness.
(Harrison, L., email).

Emily's Story

While Emily was just a small baby of probably less than six months old, we met her cousin in the shopping centre one day. Her cousin is a little girl born at the same time as my twins were due (instead of course, they had been born three months early). Emily was in my arms and she saw her cousin and just reached out to her with a look on her face as if to say, "I found you at last, so you aren't gone." It was heart breaking ...

Recently, Emily, now aged four years, came up to me and said, "Mummy, last night I had a dream and in my dream my little twin Katie didn't die, she had her lungs right and they put her in an incubator, in my incubator with me. It was so nice, Mummy." Emily is very proud of her twin and while we don't talk about her all the time she is an important member of our family. To hear Emily begin speaking of her twin like that is so special.
(Smart, R., letter).

Lisa's Story

My twin survivor Lisa is a beautiful chubby-cheeked 3 1/2 month old baby now. She was the alert one at birth. The one with the dark blue eyes that seemed to look right into the depths of my soul and this intimidated me! Amy was the peaceful baby radiating a calm quietness. Quite the opposite to Lisa, she slept most of the time.

As a result of a complicated heart defect, Amy went into heart failure on her 9th day and died when she was just 10 days old. It was during these two days that Lisa surprised me. We spent those two days in the hospital and it was as if Lisa went into hibernation. Never crying once, I had to wake her up for each feed. I would duly put her back into her carrycot where she would lie quietly until she fell asleep again. I was hardly aware of her presence at all.

Did Lisa know that Amy was dying? Did she know that I needed to conserve my strength for Amy? I believe so, because literally minutes after Amy's death, Lisa woke up and her alertness returned.

Will she feel loss in the future due to separation from her twin? This I cannot answer yet, but I will be watching her very closely!

(Louw, T., email).

Curiosity of twinship.

It is more common for a surviving twin to show curiosity about their unique situation rather than be emotionally distraught by it. If parents are aware of this, then they may feel encouraged to share their stories with their surviving twins, rather than trying to shield them from events in life that they feel may cause too much upset. Most of the time it is the parents trying to avoid the whole topic for their own sake's rather than the survivor's because they make the incorrect assumption that if bad things in life are not mentioned, then they will just go away.

It is important to remember that the survivors feel the losses too, and any questions that they ask throughout their lives, should be answered openly and honestly, with regards of course to their particular age level of understanding. And, let's face it – often children cope with life's dramas much better than adults do because they are prepared to face them, whereas adults tend to want to hide from them. Kids can teach us an awful lot about life if we let them, and they can be an immense comfort to us during times of grief.

Matthew's Story

Matt accepted that his brothers, (twin Stephen and younger brother Gavin), were in heaven and he survived to stay with us. As he has gotten older he has asked more questions and I have told him of his birth and the cause of Stephen's death. He was truly amazed and thankful of his own survival ... The most significant differences between Matthew and my other two children, (girls), ... is that he is far more reserved and does not form relationships with people as easily as the girls. (Harrison. L, email).

April's Story

April who is now 4 has always been shy and timid, and quite happy to sit back and just take things in before she gets involved. If she knows the kids and we are in a familiar place, she is fine. We quite often have characters from TV (Cartoons, etc.), in our house. She will talk and play with them as if they were here.

Only just recently April asked about Erin, (I have not actually told her she is a twin, but we have said that she has a sister and that they were in my tummy together), asked, "Where is she? Why can't we see her? Will she come back? Can we go to where she is?". She asked so many questions and was very upset when I told her that we couldn't visit Erin.

(Carlisle, N., email).

Grief causes confusion.

Grief is a time of great emotional upheaval, and confusion. It is quite common to forget things, or be unsure of something that you have just done. Try not to be fearful of this. Everyone on this planet is a special and unique individual. We therefore have vastly differing perceptions regarding life, so for some parents to say that they have observed particular behaviours in their surviving twins, and other parents to say that they have not, is not unusual. Please don't think that there is something wrong with you or your survivor because you don't fit into any of the categories mentioned above. As the following story shows, sometimes, people don't see very much at all, which is quite alright.

Matthew's Story

I think that I might try very hard to contribute; it's just a case of finding the right words to start. Matthew is just about to turn two. I know of course that it's also Jessica's birthday. We celebrate her birthday as well but to me she's not turning two like Matthew. Even though I might try and tell myself that I haven't noticed any behaviour that might indicate that he feels something is missing, when I look at things from a different perspective, (rather than just a bereaved mum), I'm sure there have been signs. Maybe I just don't want to see them, maybe one more set of 'why' questions is one too many, but I realise that they're there, and when the time comes I desperately want to be able to do and say the right thing to Matthew ... if there is a right thing.

(Mathers, J., email)

Chapter 6

DISABILITES AND OTHER CONCERNS

"To realize freedom,

the mind has to learn to look at life,

which is a vast movement

without the bondage of time,

for freedom lies beyond the field of

consciousness".

(Bruce Lee).

The increased health risks for both mother and child during a multiple pregnancy are already well documented. There is the greater chance of premature labour, risks with blood pressure, and higher infant mortality rates.

> Statistics from the National Perinatal Statistics Unit (NPSU) during 1996-98 have shown the fetal death rate in twins and other multiple births are 18.3 and 29.4 deaths per 1000. compared to 5.6 per 1000 for singleton births. (*NPSU, AIHW*, 2000).

Multiple births account for 1.5% of births, but 10.8% of perinatal mortality, (9.1% of fetal deaths and 13.9% of neonatal deaths. (*National Perinatal Statistics Unit*, 2000).

Birth of a high-order multifetal gestation is a media event, typically heralded as a technologic triumph and not reported as the serious complication of treatment that it is. The public is often left with the impression that such pregnancies turn out just fine, that they have no serious implications other than the obvious logistical and financial challenges of taking home several children at once. Those images and impressions are lasting ones that alter perspectives and influence the decisions of patients considering the same or similar treatments. (Fritz, M. A., 2000).

Other studies have revealed that

> about 20% of surviving multiples are at risk of neurological problems or delayed development if their co-multiple died in the womb ... Monochorionic (one placenta identical) surviving multiples are probably at greatest risk of problems.
>
> (Pector, E. A., Jan. 2001).

Further health problems suffered by disabled surviving twins may be lung disease, mental retardation, seizure disorders, blindness and cerebral palsy. (Jones, D., date unknown).

Coping with a disabled child is a demanding job. Therefore, trying to find important grieving time for the twin who died, must be almost impossible. Parents speak of grieving for both twins, but in a slightly different way to parents who have a survivor who is not disabled. Because of the mental and physical effort involved in looking after a disabled surviving twin, the disability becomes more of the focus, as special care is needed to ensure that the disabled child has some quality of life.

The following story reveals a part of this most private world between the mother and disabled surviving multiple:

Kate's Story

The disabled survivor has an enormous journey, and so do their parents. A journey into the unknown; where every day may bring a new challenge, a new direction and appreciation of life. A different journey; a different acceptance of life.

Grief can be complicated, the mixture of losing a precious baby, along with the loss of hopes and dreams for the survivor. ==Often the survivor needs so much care, there is little time for the natural process of grief. To separate grief for the twin that has died, and grief for the twin whose life is now headed in a different direction is not easy. "For whom do I feel what?" is often how I have felt.==

My daughter Kate has been unable to come with me on my journey with Ben. She hasn't had the natural curiosity that children have, the honesty of children's questions, she cannot articulate her feelings or thoughts of him.

And so I don't know what she thinks. She knows about him, and her eyes become large and her face becomes serious when we talk about him. At the cemetery she just stares and nods. Just recently she smiled as I left a little blue pinwheel spinning in the wind at his grave. I will never know what's inside, and so inside I quietly grieve for them both.
(Stanley. J, email)

In this chapter I have made mention of Conjoined (Siamese) twins, who face their own types of physical and in some cases mental disabilities. Parents of Conjoined twins experience not only the dilemma of whether to follow advice from medical professionals to have their children separated, knowing that there may be a greater risk that one might die, but many have to also endure interference from the media, religious groups, and 'right to life' groups.

The media view such stories as precious gems through which to sell newspapers, magazines or increase their television ratings. Right to Life groups believe that they are protecting the rights of the individual. Either way, the whole issue facing parents of Conjoined twins involves a juggling of ethical decisions by parents, doctors, religious groups, and more often than not, lawyers.

In most cases these parents find themselves in a 'no-win' situation because whatever action they choose, they will suffer some form of loss. For example, if they choose not to have the babies separated, then the children may require specialist care for the rest of their lives if they do survive. The family may feel extremely guilty, or feel that they have betrayed their twins by placing them in permanent institutional care, and thus grieve the loss of the 'normal' family unit. The family may find they lose their privacy if the unseparated Conjoined twins become the target of media attention. Not separating may keep all the religious and right-to-life groups happy, but may cause concern to the medical professionals, and eventually the parents who wonder about the future of their twins as they grow up.

If the parents choose to have the babies separated, and there is a very high risk that one, or even both could die then this may cause great upset to the parents who experience guilt for the action they have taken. There is no doubt that this may even upset all the religious and right to life groups who may complain bitterly to the media that the parents have done the wrong thing and the parents risk losing their privacy through media invasion. In both cases parents may find themselves judged by people on the street, who through reading newspaper articles or watching television news stories, feel that they have an opinion on the subject, when in fact they only know what the media has chosen to tell them.

I personally feel that each case needs to be judged independently, according to the unique situation, and should be privileged information between the parents, doctors and, if the parents wish; their religious advisors. Issues such as this type of twin loss should not become television entertainment for curious people, and lawyers should not be encouraged to sue doctors because society seems obsessed with financial compensation for every thing that goes wrong in life.

There were conflicting emotions in our own situation. We had been informed by our doctor that if our twin daughter Megan had survived, she probably would have been intellectually handicapped because of her extremely small birth weight. We therefore went through pangs of guilt for feeling relief for her that she had died, knowing full well that many intellectually handicapped people lead happy and satisfying lives.

If we consider the twin, or triplet unit as a whole, it would be a logical assumption to conclude that all the abilities, skills, attributes and personality traits that would have gone to one child, have been randomly distributed throughout the unit. This makes sense if you observe multiples and note that one may be brilliant, and the other not quite so, one's behaviour may be considered 'good' and the other regarded as 'bad', and one may possess great physical and sporting abilities, whilst the other child/ren do not.

In Rhys' case, I truly believe that if Megan had lived, she would have possessed extremely good levels in her gross motor skills, because Rhys shows very high abilities in his fine motor skills. This first became obvious in Kindergarten,

(Kindy), when the children were tested for their gross and fine motor skills. Rhys had the ability from a very young age to complete quite detailed drawings and had unusually neat handwriting for a boy; who are not generally regarded as being as neat with their handwriting skills as girls.

The Kindy staff showed great concern when they informed us of how poorly Rhys' levels were when speaking to us of his gross motor skills, such as running, balancing, and other physical activities. To be quite blunt, Rhys ran like a duck. He had no coordination whatsoever, and other children laughed at him whenever he tried to participate in sports such as cricket, football and soccer.

I remember sitting in the Murray Bridge Town Hall watching Rhys' class perform in a school concert in Primary school. The students had to dance in a skipping fashion and because of Rhys' poor abilities; it had not gone unnoticed by my husband and I, that people sitting around us were laughing at him, even though it was obvious to all how hard he was trying to get it right. As to the Kindy situation, I probably showed little concern because I truly believed that this was his share of being a twin, but it was difficult to keep explaining this to teachers because judging by the looks on their faces, they weren't too sure whether to believe me or not. Afterall, I was simply a mother, not a fully qualified and experienced schoolteacher.

The same problems continued when Rhys first began Primary School, and by the Second year I was so sick of hearing the criticisms regarding my son, that I was determined to do something positive about it. I even wrote a reply to the teacher when one of his report booklets came home, in which I stated, "It is a shame that you keep going on about the things that Rhys can't do, instead of encouraging him in what he can do." You see, everyone kept telling me that Rhys had some type of physical problem, but nobody could come up with any solutions.

One day he came home from school with a brochure about a local karate club (dojo). I enthusiastically showed the information to my husband, and we wondered whether something such as a martial art, where there is a great deal of focus and attention given to fine movements, and much practise is put into ensuring that each action is precise, would help Rhys improve with his gross motor skills. So, at age 6, Rhys started at a freestyle karate club in the rural city of Murray Bridge.

The early days were proving disastrous, and even the instructor, who eventually became a valued family friend, wondered whether this child, who seemed to possess no physical coordination whatsoever, would ever progress past the very basic stages. We fully supported Rhys, and after about six years, his coordination improved to such a great degree, that no one watching him would notice any difference between him and any other child.

Proudly, Rhys was the first student to fully complete the junior syllabus in the Murray Bridge dojo, and progressed onto the senior class where he became an Assistant Instructor. This training instilled a great sense of self-confidence in Rhys and eventually he joined the Australian Army, as able-bodied as any other individual. My son was the person to inspire me to give martial arts a try, and after 14 years as both an instructor and student, I eventually retired. However, I still appreciate, even to this day, the encouragement and support that he gave me to try something that I had wanted to try all my life, but was too scared to.

What am I therefore telling people to do? Well, as much as I would like to, I am certainly not telling everyone to enroll their surviving twin in a martial arts academy if they show a lack of physical ability, (although of course it wouldn't hurt). What I am saying is go and seek your answers if the professionals around you don't seem to have them.

Remember, as much as we would like to think so, doctors are not 'God'. Doctors can't pull rabbits out of their hats, or make all the bad things in life magically disappear. They are however, a group of extremely dedicated, experienced and well educated men and women who believe in helping others.

So, my concluding comment is, don't give up, and if it means being a bit unconventional, as in my own situation, if it works, then go for it! That is the main thing; the end result. Don't give up on your survivors because believe it or not, they don't give up on us.

Chapter 7

EFFECTS OF LOSS ON HIGHER ORDER MULTIPLES

"Do not run away; let go. Do not seek, for it will come when least expected.

(Bruce Lee).

Parents of triplets and higher order multiples can face extremely complex issues, especially when one, more or even all babies die. However it should also be noted that even in cases where all babies are born alive, there are many stresses suddenly thrust upon the family. Elizabeth Pector points out:

> It is important to understand that even when all babies are born healthy, parents of higher-order multiples experience greater financial, physical, marital and emotional stress than parents of singletons or twins, with higher rates of depression and divorce. Disability rates are significantly higher in sets of triplets, quadruplets and more. Loss rates are also correspondingly higher, and quadruplet and higher pregnancies are particularly at high risk of fetal loss, premature delivery, and/or health problems for the mother. (Pector, E., 2002).

What is interesting, but perhaps not all that surprising, are the feelings experienced by survivors from a triplet, or higher order pregnancy. Their emotions echo those of the surviving

==twin, although I do believe that the situation is exacerbated because of the greater number of individuals involved.==

One adult sole survivor was asked how they felt about being a triplet, having come from a home where the subject was rarely approached. This was her reply:

> I feel blessed, that only for a brief time, God blessed me with their presence. Even though I don't remember any part of my inutero experience, I do feel a loss most times when I'm thinking of all the fun we could have had fooling people. My sister Anna Nichole, was identical to me, or so my Mom says. I feel sad most times to know they're not with me, but I do know that they're with my Lord and Saviour Jesus Christ, and they are without pain. (Rublee, S. M., email).

The same surviving triplet commented upon the difficulties in forming friendships, which again, can be regarded as very similar to that of a surviving twin.

> As I was growing up I wasn't the most popular, so I didn't have many friends, but when I had the chance I always looked for people to follow. I always felt that I was more of a follower than a leader. Possibly my sister Anna, or brother Neal would have been the leader. As an adult I have grown up a bit and asserted myself more in situations, and making friends, but I still don't feel a true leader. (Rublee, S. M., email).

Survivors too speak of an intense loneliness without their other siblings. Sometimes they find daily tasks difficult because they feel lost, and unable to fit in with the rest of the world. They quite often look for a 'replacement'. Perhaps not consciously, but they still seek to fill an unfillable void just the same. As mentioned in the Chapter, Common Survivor Behaviour, my son Rhys tended to, over the years, end up with close friends who were the same sex and age as his deceased twin would have been.

My parents had a Polaroid picture taken of each sibling and I have often looked at them and felt a huge loss, and wished they were there with me because I feel so lonely. Most times I can't go to the store alone, it's like a big part of me is missing. I've found different types of friends to fill the voids; like I picture my sister to be a great friend, someone I would tell anything, share my every moment with.

I picture my brother to be a pain and always want to pick on me, but love me just the same. And I picture him to have a strong bond to my sister and I also ... kinda like the Three Musketeers! (Rublee, S. M., email).

The comments regarding this survivor's brother especially reveal that survivors do still possess a sense of humour, despite all that has occurred. And they do try very hard to understand how their parents feel, and even why their parents prefer not to mention what has occurred in the past. As this survivor mentions,

> I understand why they, (the parents), don't speak about it, it would hurt especially since my mother was only 22 or 23 when we were born'. (Rublee, S. M., email).

By contrast, it is good to understand the parental viewpoint in triplet loss issues. When asked how they view their surviving triplets, some parents have responded by saying,

> I definitely feel like a piece of the puzzle is missing. I feel like my boys are missing out because if she were here, their experience would be so unique, so different than the one they have now. (Ruiz. J., email).

or comments such as,

> The loss is still the same no matter a twin, triplet or other. I do believe that it is harder to deal with higher multiple loss but only in different place, i.e. my daughters looked very similar. We do not know if they could have been identical. I

> am reminded every day of what "I don't" have. This would be true also of identical and to some degree fraternal twins. However, and this is my humble opinion, this makes no difference with the loss. While I am reminded every day of what I don't have, others may relish in the joy of what they do have ... these are the degrees. (Wilder. M., email).

One parent also noted the similarities between twin and triplet loss, but acknowledged the significance of the particular loss when there is an increase in numbers of survivors, creating an extremely complex and as she put it, 'multi-faceted' situation.

> I would imagine that my children do go through the same behavioural patterns as surviving twins. However, there is one very significant twist. As with my daughter, she is missing her sister, my son is missing his sister, but they have each other.
> (Wilder. M., email).

As mentioned previously, it is common for surviving twins, or sole surviving higher order multiples to look for companions who are similar to their deceased sibling/s. It would therefore be a logical assumption that two surviving triplets for example, would form an even stronger bond with each other, rather than seek the company of another person. But, perhaps in a desperate effort to correct the now unbalanced triplet or other multiple-order picture, this does not always occur.

> I find that my daughter does not necessarily go to my son for comfort. However, for protection, (as much as a six year old can), she does look to him, (i.e. at school, etc.). My daughter does seem to gravitate towards my oldest daughter rather than her brother for play, (or their nine year old cousin who lives next door).

> As with my son, he gravitates towards my youngest daughter who is only fourteen months younger. It would appear that they were developmentally the same, so he might have felt less threatened. (Wilder. M., email).

Early in the preface I have spoken about the way those around us view our survivors, and the pain for parents who raise surviving twins when they are recognised as singletons, and triplets who are referred to as twins. One mother raising two surviving triplets reinforced this observation:

> A twin on the other hand, while never being a true singleton, is viewed as such, and almost expected to act as such, (to some degree). My survivors are to act as twins, (which of course they are not). (Wilder. M, email).

Another mother of two surviving triplets shared her feelings regarding the same subject:

> It hurts because all they see is two, when I know there should be three. This is hardest when we are with triplet friends and they get showered with attention, and they look at me as if having two is "no big deal". I think even close friends have a hard time identifying them as "triplets" since my boys happen to also be identical twins. (Ruiz. J, email).

One mother who lost her only female triplet expressed deep anger at comments made by people who find it difficult to understand:

> Everything would've been different if she had lived. I changed the entire nursery to be very masculine once she passed away. It had been pink and light blue gingham, but now it is denim with a sports theme. My house is dedicated to trucks and balls, and cars. If she were here there would be dollys and a kitchen set. The boys would be exposed to those things.
>
> I feel like our lives would be richer because of her presence. I wouldn't have to live everyday with that void. I wouldn't have to try and figure out how we can afford another IVF cycle in order to try again. Life would be harder with another child, but easier because I wouldn't know this pain.
>
> Someone once said to me, "Two out of three isn't bad". Well, it is bad, because it should've been three out of three. No one gets pregnant, gives birth, and then plans on

> returning everything and planning a funeral, just so that on special days they can go visit their child that lies beneath a patch of grass! Sorry, as you can see, even after two and a half years, the anger still shows up. I do have a lot of anger because our daughter was the healthiest of the three since she had her own placenta. (Ruiz. J, email).

Behavioural traits such as fascination with mirrors, as with many twin survivors, seemed to be another common element to triplet survivors. One family did notice that the two young surviving triplet boys showed interest in colours commonly associated with girls. This can be of significance when one is reminded that the deceased triplet was a girl.

> I think they "miss" her in their own way. They love mirrors, but I've also noticed that they are drawn to pink things. I think because we don't have any in our home other than her memorabilia. They see it as an interesting colour because of its absence. They also love little girls their age; shy around

them, but can't stop staring, whereas they just play with boys their age. (Ruiz. J, email).

The same mother of two surviving triplets commented that

They love our multiples playgroup, and play quite nicely with those kids, but at the church playgroup where everyone is a singleton, they only play with each other. (Ruiz. J, email).

In the Chapter, Common Survivor Behaviour, one of the mothers of the surviving twins speaks about unexplainable events that appear to border upon the supernatural. To my great surprise and interest, one of the surviving triplet mothers, who lives on the opposite side of the world, also mentioned her own experience with such events. Although not generally revealed by parents, I assume mostly from the fear of being ridiculed instead of taken seriously, it is interesting to note the responses of both families.

Neither family appears frightened, or 'spooked' by these occurrences. Instead they tell of finding comfort, and truly feel that the spirits of their deceased children are not far away. One family emailed me a Christmas photo which, (unbeknown to the person who took the photo at the time), happened to include a portion of the television screen in the background.

Whether it is a result of the film and the flickering television screen, no one can be absolutely sure, but as the mother points out, the shape of the ghostly figure that appears, resembles an angel. This mother concluded her story by telling me that, we also have toys turn off and on by themselves all of the time. I feel she is always with us. (Ruiz. J, email).

A story regarding the behavioural patterns of the survivors at or around the time of the death of the other sibling, also reveal a similar thread to behavioural patterns of some surviving twins.

On the actual day Cecilia died, the boys were also in the neo-intensive care unit in the room right next to hers. It was their worst day there. The nurses told me about how while we were saying our goodbyes from 3-3.20, the boys were just plain inconsolable! I truly believe that they felt what was happening. They knew a big part of them was leaving them.

It hurts to still think of their reaction. But the nurses said it was almost as if they were in physical pain. It was the only day they ever behaved this way during their almost two month stay in the NICU. I also wanted to add that although they don't have much awareness yet of their angel sister, one of their first words was 'angel', because we say goodnight to her every night.

They have a weird reaction whenever one or the other is gone for a while, i.e. sleeping in our room, not in his crib. They almost have an inborn response of fear that something is missing. They start searching for the other and get on the verge of crying when they call out their brother's name and there is no response. It just pains me when they do this. I have to go show the awake child that the other one is okay and he goes off to play. It's almost like they're scared to lose another piece of the puzzle. (Ruiz. J, email).

Therefore to conclude that there is great similarity between twin loss and higher order multiple loss, would be absolutely correct. It is most important however, that the more complex issues regarding numbers of survivors, as well as grieving issues created by increases in deceased siblings, should be given careful consideration. Families should be shown respect, and understanding, without being patronized and pitied.

Multiple Birth Loss Families & Grief

"Twin loss families have stated that some medical staff, friends and family may ignore the child or children who have died because they feel this increases the pain for the bereaved family. Ignoring the deceased multiple birth child/ren can actually increase the pain and make it difficult for the surviving multiple birth child/ren to feel comfortable with their position in life."

(Used with permission from the NTLS brochure 'Coping with Twin Loss')

Chapter 8

SHOULD I TELL THE TRUTH?

"If you bury your grief, your grief will bury you."

(Harold E. Jones).

A resounding "Yes" always springs into my mind whenever I hear parents of surviving twins ask if they should be honest with their survivor about his or her unique status in life. I have counselled too many parents over the years to think otherwise. Being honest has worked well in my own particular situation and I believe there is no reason why it shouldn't work with other families.

Elizabeth Pector reminds us of an extremely valid point in not placing the dead twin on a pedestal, making the image for the survivor difficult to 'live up to';

> It is important to avoid idealizing the child who died. In this regard, referring to a 'guardian angel" or "angel twin" might have some negative impact on the surviving twin whose behaviour is less than angelic. Many parents believe their deceased child's spirit is guiding their survivor, and I myself have referred to my deceased son being "with the angels and God." However, as children get older and understand our words, we should make sure we're not

unintentionally conveying the message that the deceased child is perfect or better than the child who lived. (Pector, E. A., Jan. 2001).

Generally, people might make the incorrect assumption that young children don't understand many of life's complexities and that they are better simply not knowing. They feel that it would cause too much upset, and that because the dead twin is not around anymore, that the child is best forgotten.

As previously mentioned in the chapter, "Common Survivor Behaviour", children are more resilient and intelligent than many of us might like to think. If we are prepared to present the story on their level, that is, in terms that they would understand at their particular age, most families would find that younger children are more curious about their twinship, than upset by it. Besides making them feel special, it may assist in helping some to also understand why they sometimes feel distant and aloof from the rest of the world.

In her professional capacity, Elizabeth Pector made a very important and valid statement in a letter to the editor of a United States magazine aimed at medical professionals. She reminded colleagues of the risks associated with multiple pregnancies. These were some of her comments that are well worth noting by both medical professionals and parents alike:

> I wish to remind my colleagues that multiple pregnancies carry a significantly higher risk of morbidity and mortality for both the mother and the infants, and that issues in grieving the loss of pregnancy in multiple gestations are misunderstood.
>
> With the rising number of twin pregnancies … it is important that physicians not minimize the grief process that parents undergo when either a "selective reduction" procedure is undertaken or an accidental loss occurs early or late in a multiple pregnancy. In particular, attempts to reassure parents that they "at least" have one or more

survivors from the pregnancy will damage the physician's relationship with them. (Pector, E.A., Dec. 1998).

Over many years, Joan Woodward interviewed numerous surviving twins who had been separated from their womb mates at varying stages of life; at birth, in childhood and adulthood. It was upon either being informed about their twinship, or accidentally discovering it, that many spoke of finding a sense of belonging in knowing where they really were. It answered a lot of previously unanswered questions.

> ==I still maintain that it is the attitude of the parents of the surviving twin that has the most profound effect on their feelings concerning themselves.== This seems particularly true when the truth about being a twin has been withheld and when they feel devalued as a lone twin for whatever reason.

Parents struggling to manage their own grief, perhaps unable to speak of it, or, as time goes by monopolizing it within the family, tends to leave the surviving twin suffering a deep sense of isolation. (Woodward, J., 1999).

Some mothers are pressured to keep their 'secret' of two babies. This pressure may come from both doctors, as well as well-meaning relatives who may feel that it is better to not mention some of the 'unpleasant things' that life throws up at us.

This holds true especially for some of the previous generations where societal views were very different towards mothers who delivered stillborn children. The war years created a difficult and unrealistic perspective towards death, where it became so common that people developed an almost blasé attitude towards what was an almost daily occurrence. There was no time to grieve – people just had to get on with the obligations and rituals of everyday life.

However, to bottle up grief doesn't work.

> Attempting to avoid grieving … doesn't work! Like sweeping the dirt under the mat, the pain and reality will still be visible there, just as soon as someone lifts up the corner. (Schulz, L., Dec. 1998).

I have counselled women who have tried to pretend that nothing happened, for up to twenty years. Suddenly something happens in life which brings the memories flooding back. These women sometimes require hospitalisation and professional psychiatric care in order to go back to the very beginning and grieve for the twin who has died. Then they have to cope with telling the survivor.

I know of women who suffered singleton stillbirths, and tried to keep their losses hidden away. Years later some suffered 'nervous breakdowns', were carted off to psychiatric hospitals, and given Electro-Convulsive Therapy, (or electric shock treatment), to "help" them cope. It makes me all the more conscious of the importance of honesty within multiple pregnancy losses.

There have been other situations where the survivors have discovered they have a twin by accident, perhaps after the death of a parent when they are required to sort through paperwork. I know of one instance where the surviving twin was accidentally told during a casual conversation with a family friend who, (nineteen years later), forgot to keep the secret. It pays in the long term to be honest with our survivors because they will eventually discover who they really are, and let's face it – it's not fair to make everyone we know have to remember for the rest of their lives to not say anything about a difficult situation that belongs to us.

As parents, we may genuinely feel that we have our surviving twins' best interests in mind when making the decision not to tell them about their twin ship. However, if we are to be truly empathetic with our survivors, it is important to see the picture from their point of view. As one lone twin from Joan Woodward's study shares;

> At one point I might have chosen the word 'incomplete' to sum up my experience of being a lone twin. I felt like a jigsaw puzzle which had one piece missing and this piece was the key to the whole picture. Feeling more positive, I am now able to focus on the nearly completed puzzle and not merely see that part which is missing.

I accept that I cannot change the fact that my family of origin is unable to speak of my brother and that his death remains a taboo subject. They can neither recognise, acknowledge, respect nor encourage my need to speak out. I feel that this silence serves to deny his existence; as we developed together for thirty-five precious weeks, I wonder about the significance of this. In the context of my home, church and friends I have found the freedom to break the silence. (Woodward, J., 1999).

It is important that we acknowledge that by sharing the truth and being honest with our surviving twins, we can find a balance between a healthy reality and an unhealthy obsession. So, let's allow our wonderful surviving twins the chance to celebrate their unique position in this world, instead of treating it with shame. Let's refuse to hide under the heavy blanket of societal fear, guilt and other emotional burdens that plague us, and fling them off to reveal the shining lights of joy and love that our children can truly bring us, if we only find the courage to let them.

Chapter 9

MEMORY TRIGGERS

"Fear is that little darkroom where negatives are developed".

(Michael Pritchard).

Memory triggers are the emotional and physical reminders of our loss and can, to a lesser degree, start the whole grieving process again. They are a normal part of life and if acknowledged and recognised, can be more easily dealt with.

> Memory triggers", such as birthdays, Christmas, and other anniversaries, can take a person back a stage or two. (Schulz, L., Dec. 1998)

especially during the early years. As the years pass, these reminders may wax and wane. Some events may trigger a more severe reaction than others. As life introduces new experiences to us a memory may be suddenly and unexpectedly triggered.

Major events in any child's life, such as beginning kindergarten, or starting primary or high school should be associated with feelings of happiness and joy. However, for families with surviving twins, these events can cruelly remind them of that 'missing' part of the twin picture, i.e. the twin who has died. Discovering intact sets of multiples within your survivor's class at school can be quite a shock, and it is easier if teachers are aware and therefore sensitive to, the feelings of the surviving twin and his or her family.

Julie Bryant, and two of her colleagues have collated a list of suggested questions in the form of a letter, that parents may like to give to staff caring for their young child or school teachers in order to help them better care for the needs of surviving multiple children. Without making a huge issue of the situation, make the care-giver or teacher aware of the fact that the surviving child or children was/were born as a set of twins/triplets/quadruplets, etc., but one or more died during pregnancy, at birth or shortly after. A letter written to the staff is an excellent way in which to approach this delicate emotional situation because it can be kept on file for future reference. The following is just one example of a suggested letter that you could send to your child's kindy, school, or give to their care provider. Try to keep the length to no more than one page if possible, and encourage the person to whom it is given, to add it to your child's file for easy reference:

SAMPLE LETTER TO TEACHER/CARE PROVIDER.

Dear (teacher's/care provider's name),

This letter serves to introduce (child's name) who is a surviving twin/triplet/quadruplet. Surviving multiple children often display traits considered as accepted normal behaviour within multiple birth groups. However, some of these behaviours, (such as keeping to themselves), may cause concern if the child is incorrectly viewed as a singleton.

Sometimes surviving multiples will display extremes in their physical and mental abilities, and may show this by displaying above-average abilities in some skills, whilst showing extreme difficulties with others. They may also occasionally reveal signs associated with grief.

Authorities in the area of multiple loss recognise that the most devastating forms of loss are the ones occurring within the first six years of life. It will greatly assist (child's name) if you could be sensitive and empathic to his/her emotional needs as they arise. This will help (child's name) in building self-confidence and in feeling comfortable with his/her own identity.

Many adult survivors speak of feeling isolated and having difficulty in finding their own place within the world. Early positive intervention has shown to be beneficial to both survivor and their immediate family in making this journey less stressful and confusing.

If any particular behaviours cause worry or concern, please do not hesitate to contact me on (phone number), so that we may discuss the issue to ensure the situation falls within a realistic parameter.

Thanking you for your cooperation and understanding with this matter.

Yours sincerely
(Parent's name and signature)

In some childcare and educational facilities, staff may initially show some reluctance to cooperate with your requests, simply because there is very little awareness of twin loss and higher order loss situations. With gentle but persistent persuasion, staff should be encouraged to bring any particular observations or concerns about your survivor/s's development to you for discussion, to ensure that it falls within accepted multiple birth behavioural patterns. As Julie points out:

- Your child/ren may tend to identify more with other multiple-birth children
- Your child/ren may also tend to prefer their own company in a group activity or play situation. They may appear to be 'off in their own little world' but be mindful that if they had their birth sibling/s by their side this would be perceived differently
- They may also form a strong bond with one other person (especially if your child is the sole survivor) and this may be their way of

subconsciously filling the void of not having their birth sibling/s by their side

- You may want to mention that in your family situation you are doing all you can to ensure your child/ren have a healthy and balanced understanding of themselves as a surviving child/ren in a multiple birth

- In those very early childhood years, your intuition may tell you that because of your child/ren's multiple birth status, they will need to be 'socialised' early with other children

- As your child/ren becomes aware of their deceased birth sibling/s they may want to communicate their feelings to their day-care staff/school teachers. Likewise they may want to tell their friends. This may be communicated conversationally, in play (e.g. with an imaginary friend), in story telling, writing, picture drawing

- Ask the day-care staff/school teachers to encourage this awareness as a unique aspect of who your surviving child/ren are and that this is their way of 'coming to terms'. Your child/ren will need to be believed when they speak about their deceased birth sibling/s to ensure that what they say is not written-off as a vivid imagination.

- Your surviving child/ren may benefit from one on one attention from the teacher, for eg. Putting their required work a bit 'out of reach' to make them strive for higher goals. This may help with confidence. Your child/ren's academic results and personal development may be hampered if just left or ignored.

(Bryant, J, email).

Our own family experiences within the school system have varied from year to year, and have been partially dependent upon the teacher's ability to empathise with our son. I am sharing my experiences so that parents can be informed and hopefully not be discouraged because a particular teacher does not appear to be receptive towards the topic of twin loss issues.

One year Rhys had a teacher who was very observant of her students. She and Rhys got along extremely well and she was impressed with his high level of intelligence for a child of his age. She also told us how much she valued the friendship that they had developed during the year. She further commented during parent/teacher interview evening how Rhys seemed to be treated differently by his fellow classmates. "Not in a nasty way", she told us. His behaviour fascinated more than concerned her.

This teacher noted that students sometimes physically moved away from Rhys, but he was well liked in his class and mixed well with the other children. Reactions by class members didn't seem to bother Rhys, who is generally more upset if one of his immediate family is unkind to him, rather than someone from school. There was something 'different' about him that she couldn't quite pick out. We agreed and congratulated her on being a very observant woman. In that situation we simply smiled to ourselves and didn't feel the need to say anything about Rhys' twinship.

The next year was vastly different, with a teacher who had previously taught my husband many years earlier at the local high school. Rhys' teacher began the interview by stating that she felt that there were emotional problems with him, and strongly suggested counselling. She was very concerned that he didn't seem to have any strong friendships within his class, and that he tended to be a loner, keeping to himself more often than not.

These comments were enough to make me explode, which I unfortunately, proceeded to do. I failed dismally in keeping calm and objective; immediately telling this teacher that Rhys was quite normal for a surviving twin, and that he definitely didn't require counselling. My voice became loud and shrill and the teacher began to look at me like I was some type of crazy woman who was desperately in need of professional psychiatric care; and perhaps at the time, she may have been correct.

However, as I am sure that we have all lost our tempers at one time or another; I continued to rant at this woman, who was only sharing her professional opinion as a teacher with me. Thankfully, my now ex-husband, was with me at the time. He was able to portray a much calmer disposition; gently guiding me towards the door.

Looking back I can honestly compare myself with a two year old child throwing a tantrum in the middle of a supermarket lolly-aisle. Here I was, a grown woman, being slowly dragged out of a small classroom, screaming like a banshee at a teacher who was not remotely interested in anything being said. The teacher didn't appear to care that I did a great deal of work in the area of twin loss issues. She didn't seem to care that I had founded a twin loss charity. She didn't even seem to care that I was recognised overseas! She was probably more concerned, (and rightly so), that I was going to spoil her timetable of parent-teacher interviews that night.

Although I didn't tell anyone else about the experience, I must confess that when the teacher died of cancer several years later, I felt a twinge of guilt. I felt I could have handled that parent-teacher interview night in a more grown-up fashion. I felt disappointed that we were unable to find some common ground upon which to discuss the topic of twin loss issues in a more objective and appropriate manner.

Ironically, instead of Rhys seeing the school counsellor, I made an appointment for myself the very next day. Sometimes living in a country town has its advantages, as well as its disadvantages. Through business and social circles, the school's counsellor knew me well enough to know that I didn't usually perform tantrums like a two year old, or scream like a banshee at school teachers. We spoke at length about Rhys and twin loss issues, and by the time I left his office, the counsellor was standing at the door waving goodbye, saying that he was going to purchase a copy of my first book, "The Diary".

The school counsellor had found our conversation extremely interesting and educational. He had no concerns about Rhys whatsoever, and could see that although at this point in time he did not have many close friends his own age, he possessed a great many friends of all ages, through our church, family and social circles.

Society can be extremely hurtful in how it views surviving twins because of the extra attention given to intact set of multiples. These can be viewed as a 'novelty item', especially when their parents dress them the same. There are stories published in newspapers, women's magazines, and flashed on the television. These families for a brief moment at least, find themselves treated like celebrities and are even recognised in public. Parents of intact higher order multiples may even receive free gifts from the community such as food hampers, furniture, cars and new houses. So, you can understand the extreme devastation and humiliation that families who suffer losses within a multiple pregnancy quite often feel. They are robbed of the children that they so desperately wanted, and they lose their status within society.

> When your twins are alive, people fuss and tell you how clever you are. When one dies, it seems there is a silent reject stamp on your forehead and they secretly call you a total failure. (Schulz, L., Dec. 1998).

In Rhys' situation, his Baptism for example, should have been a day of celebration and joy. It turned out to be a day of conflicting emotions and unwanted reminders;

> Rhys' baptism; it should have been Megan's too. It is April Fool's Day and it feels like I have been the victim of some sadistic joke. It is difficult to stand up in front of the huge church congregation to present our son and not suddenly

start crying. I hold back the tears – it is very hard. I ache inside. I feel lost and empty – but I feel loving and proud of Rhys. It is Rhys who helps to keep us going. (Schulz, L., Dec. 1998).

Our family is sensitive to Rhys' need to celebrate his birthday in a positive, happy family environment. The days have passed where he watched his mother cry over a gravesite every year. He feels proud to be a twin and we therefore try hard to create more memorable activities to affirm this.

The following activities are useful in celebrating the lives of both twins, (and higher order multiples), and helping the survivor to feel proud of his or her twinship:

- releasing helium filled balloons for the number of years being celebrated
- planting a special tree, rose bush or some other favourite shrub

- visiting the gravesite with flowers and cards to sing a birthday song
- listening to some special music
- making a double cake. (Rhys chose to have a double cake for his tenth birthday, without any prompting from us).
- making lanterns and floating them down the river. (This we did for Rhys'/Megan's twenty-first birthday/anniversary).

Up to this point, I have referred to memory triggers as mainly being a series of events that can bring back the grief. However, I feel it is important to note that what people say can have the same, dramatic and startling effect. Remember back in chapter 1, where I spoke about the 'power of words', and how they can build us up, as well as tear us down? Well, there are times when those around us mention something, or say something, not intentionally hurtful, that can bring back all the sadness, and remind us of what we have lost.

An example that tends to haunt me is when family, friends and acquaintances remark upon the fact that I 'only have boys'. It is a sharp sting of cruel reality when a person states, "You're lucky you don't have any girls in your family!" Although I dumbly nod my head in agreement, it feels like a verbal 'kick in the teeth', that is, kicking someone whilst they are lying on the ground, helpless and unable to defend themselves. These days I don't often respond. It would only add to the embarrassment of the comment. However, sometimes I do respond quietly with the line, "my daughter died", just to listen to the silence.

This doesn't mean that your family and friends have to watch every single word they say to you for the rest of their lives because you are a bereaved parent. It doesn't mean that they have to feel like they're 'walking on eggshells', uncomfortable in having a casual conversation for fear of saying something to upset someone. I just want people to be aware of what they say, and how they say it, and be more sensitive to other's unique and perhaps painful situations.

Memory triggers can be a real shock to families who feel that they have recovered from their initial grieving period. Unless they are made aware of them, parents may feel that they have not yet fully come to terms with, or 'resolved' their grief for the twin who has died, even though a number of years have passed. As it is quite acceptable to remember happy times with a laugh, so it is more than acceptable to remember the sad times with a tear.

The most important thing to remember is that grieving is not a stagnant, solid entity. It is a flexible, constantly changing life experience.

> It is quite common for a grieving person to spend many months, sometimes years, jumping back and forth from stage to stage. Some stages can haunt us for the rest of our

lives, but as long as you are the one to control your grief, not the grief controlling you, then you can generally be sure that you're a survivor! (Schulz, L., Dec. 1998).

One of my twins died.

Am I still the mother of twins?

"Often health care professionals, in their attempts to try and lessen parental grief, will say the surviving child is no longer a twin, but this is incorrect. Psychological studies show that many surviving multiple birth children struggle throughout life, battling emotions of isolation, having trouble forming long-term relationships, and wondering why they feel 'different' from the rest of the world."

(Used with permission from the NTLS brochure 'Questions from parents')

Chapter 10

CULTURE AND MYSTERY

"If a man does not keep pace with his companions, perhaps it is because he hears a different drummer. Let him step to the music which he hears, however measured or far away".

(Henry David Thoreau).

From a sociological aspect, 'culture' is regarded as knowledge, values, beliefs, attitudes, language, symbols and customs that are common to a particular society. These components give the individual members of that society a basis on which to form their lives. The components of a culture differ from one to the next, making each one unique. Most perceptions relating to twinship that I have discussed in this book, are generally based on Western societal viewpoints. However, it is interesting, (and sometimes frightening), to note the beliefs of other cultures in this particular area.

In some past primitive societies, where the search for food and shelter were the primary daily concern, twins were considered a liability because two babies required sustenance from the one mother, at the one time. Therefore, because of the harsh realities of life, twin births were viewed as bad luck and the weakest twin was killed to give at least one twin a chance of survival. (*Twin Majority*, 2002).

To most of us, this would appear to be an extremely cruel and unthinkable act, but to these types of societies, this behaviour was just a fact of life. It is difficult to not want to judge one culture by another one's beliefs, but thankfully, not all cultures viewed twin births in this way.

In Nigeria, the Yoruba people considered twins to be 'good spirits' because twins were associated with mystical and magical forces. (Hunt, S., May 1997).

This society therefore regarded twins as sacred, bringing good luck to the family, and giving reason for great celebration amongst the whole tribe.

> Twinning as a biological phenomenon is exceptionally common among the Yoruba. Forty-five births in 1000 are twins. This is a rate of twinning which is four times that of either the United States or Great Britain. Parents of twins greet their birth as both a blessing and a burden. Twins double everything. They are twice as much trouble, but

> bring twice as much good fortune to those parents who give them proper care. ...

> The association of twins with the spirit world is somewhat more abstract than their association with the wild and erratic Bush. Twins ... share a common soul. For some Yoruba they are also ... destined to die. Twins bridge the gap between the world of the gods and the world of humans. (Ulrich. G., 1996)

In the Yoruba culture it is considered improper and even dangerous to say that a twin has died, because of the link between the spirit and human world, so people say that the deceased child has

> gone to Lagos (the major city of Nigeria) to make a fortune for the family. ... Special rituals, songs and dances associated with living twins must be continued after death with even greater adherence to prescription. (Ulrich. G., 1996)

According to religious custom, mothers commission carvings to be made of the deceased twin to ensure that the direct contact between both worlds is not broken. The Yoruba are the only West African people to undertake such ritual.

In stark contrast, some of the Native American Indian tribes thought twins were harbingers of evil brought about by sinister powers. (Hunt, S., May 1997).
Their fear and ignorance of the unknown meant that, sadly, both twins were usually killed at birth.

Beth Pector has done a great deal of research into the relationship between twins and culture. She states that

> Cultural beliefs about the nature of multiples appear in the mourning practices of many civilizations. Ethnographic literature suggests common themes that echo modern concepts. Many societies viewed twins as fragile, likely to die without preferential or meticulously equal treatment. A

shared soul between twins is a common tenet, and the death of one is often felt to herald the other's prompt demise. The close relationship between multiples influences funerary rites. Honor, fear and mysticism are often evident in rituals. Twin infanticide was widely practiced, yet mourning customs were still observed. Many peoples recognise the special status of multiples and their families after one, two or more die. (Pector, E., Jun. 2002).

There is such a diversity of cultural and religious beliefs and practices within our world. In fact,

> Everything we do, every decision we make and course of action we take is based on our consciously and unconsciously chosen beliefs, attitudes and values. (Warland, J., 2000).

Jane Warland also points out the cultural diversity surrounding death and burial:

> Many cultures have important religious rites to be observed at or around the time of death. These may include baptism, blessing or 'last rites'. Usually an ordained minister of the religion will attend to perform the rite. ... Some religions have strict rules as to who may touch a dead body. ...
>
> Adherents of some religions are forbidden to agree to an autopsy. In other cases an autopsy can be performed but it must be according to strict guidelines about what goes on during and after the autopsy. ... Some faiths require that the internment occurs quickly after the death. (Warland, J., 2000).

Ceremonies and adherence to particular rites, are still widely practiced during and after a baby's birth. Baptism rites for example are common religious practices that vary greatly according to a person's belief and culture.

Twinship is surrounded by a great deal of mysticism. It is common for twins to act in a similar manner, share the same tastes in clothing, food, friends, and even complete their other sibling's sentences during a conversation. There are countless stories of twins who have been separated by distance either at a young age, or during adulthood, behaving in exactly the same manner. Medical science still has no real understanding of some twin behaviours regarding death and burial. Therefore the whole concept of twinship continues to be shrouded in mystical, magical, even romantic notions.

Some of the world's most famous people were surviving twins. One of the best known was Elvis Presley, whose twin brother Jessie was stillborn on January 1935. Sadly, very little, apart from a few lines here and there, is written about Presley's twinship. My assumption is that in 1935 it was considered more correct to say nothing. Societal opinion of the day would have been to just forget, move on with life, and avoid any unnecessary upset and emotional pain.

Another famous surviving twin, best known in the motorcycle world for his land speed record set on an Indian Scout, was New Zealand man, Burt Munro. Burt, was born in Invercargill in 1899, and died in 1978. His twin sister had died at birth. Once again, true to his generation at the time, not much is known about Burt's sister. However, Burt was recorded as stating that the doctor didn't hold much hope for him either when he was born, saying that he wouldn't live past two years of age!

During the Second World War when the Nazis rounded up Jews for slaughter, Dr Josef Mengele showed an unhealthy obsession with twins. Fascinated by them he used hundreds of twins in cruel and sickening medical experiments, ranging from injecting chemicals into children's eyes to see if their eyes would change colour, to sewing a set of Gypsy twins together back to back in an effort to create his very own Conjoined twins.

In the Auschwitz death camp during the mid nineteen forties, twins were

> Mengle's favourite subjects, and they were afforded special treatment, such as being able to keep their own hair and clothing, and receiving extra food rations. As long as they stayed healthy and useful to Mengele, they would be kept alive.
> (Bulow, L., 2002).

The famous American author Samuel Clemens, (better known as Mark Twain), also held an obsession with twins, although thankfully, a less gruesome one than Josef Mengele. He mostly focused his preoccupation upon a set of Conjoined Twins known as the 'Tocci brothers', who basically inspired Twain to write great and creative literature.

Ancient Iranians followed the teachings of an Eastern Gnostic named Mani, who held his own particular views regarding twinship. He believed that every man had a spiritual 'double' with whom he or she would be united with after death.

Rachel Ndi, has done extensive studies of the culture of twins in her region of West Africa. She sums up the whole issue of twinship in the following manner:

> Many cultures, including our own, celebrate the birth of twins, some view them as something dangerous that must be destroyed but it is rare to find a society that is indifferent to this unusual occurrence. The treatment of twins in West Africa is particularly unusual, possibly due to the high twin rate in this area. In the Cameroonian Grassfields twins are generally regarded as gifts from God. They are highly celebrated and respected. My own experience as a 'Manyi" (mother of twins) in Cameroonian culture made me aware of the significance of twins in this society.
> (Ndi, R., 2000).

Some of the most interesting beliefs held by the Kpe people of the Cameroon area of Africa included the rituals undergone by a pregnant woman to ensure that she had a healthy pregnancy. These rituals also included attempting to prevent the production of twins, not because these people disliked twins, but because of the concern for the mother having to care for frail babies, and the problems associated with a twin birth.

It was also commonly believed that twins did not like the homes into which they had been born, and that is why many of them chose to die. There was also the fear that if you gave something to one twin and not the other, you would offend the twin who did not receive the particular item or gift, and cause a life threatening situation for that child.

Twins who died in infancy were buried in mwendene leaves, which grow quite large. The idea behind this was that this would stop the children from being born again because the Kpe believed that some children belong to the underworld and are born just to vex their parents by dying in infancy again and again. (Ndi, R., 2000).

When a twin dies in the Oku kingdom,

it is buried as fast as possible with two leafless neck garlands. If one is living, it is given salt and oil and the twin rite is performed. If both die before the ritual, then they are buried with no ceremony. The Oku do not believe in reincarnation and once a child is dead it is gone. At birth the placentas are buried in two separate but adjacent graves, if the twins die at this time the placentas are still buried but are buried at the (1)*twin specialist's home while the twins are buried at the father's home. (Ndi, R., 2000).

When a twin dies in infancy in Bali,

the body is taken far into the bush and left sitting upright on a rock with props to keep the twin in place. The bearers then run as fast as they can from the place without looking back. (Ndi, R., 2000).

As the influence of a Christian Western society has permeated throughout most other cultures, many of the rituals that have been mentioned in this chapter are probably no longer followed. If they still are, it is a good assumption that these cultural rites are not followed as strictly as they would have been many years ago, or have been greatly modified to suit the changing society.

It would also be logical to conclude that many of the past practises of some of the previously mentioned groups, (such as those who chose to kill either one or both twins at birth), would now be highly illegal in the eyes of most modern Western judicial systems around the world.

Author's note: (1) *twin specialist is the local village medical practitioner or midwife who has experience in handling twin pregnancies and births.

Chapter 11

THE FUTURE?

"Even though I don't remember my siblings, the only thing I can hang onto is my gift of salvation, knowing that Jesus Christ sacrificed himself on the cross to pay for my sins, and that one day, I will see my sister and brother again. Even though I've never met you Anna and Neal, I love you, and you'll live in my heart forever and one day we'll be together again. Love your sister, Shannon."

(Rublee, S. M., email)

If family and friends are positive in their approach towards bereavement care, then this affects our survivors in a positive manner also. Instead of being ashamed, or embarrassed by our unique family situations, we should be celebrating and sharing them with all those around us. As one adult surviving twin stated, "You're a twin for life", (Allman. P, *email*),
and that's the simple fact of the matter.

Some survivors suffer the guilt of being just that – a survivor. Just as war veterans and accident victims have to fight the emotional conflict within, so too do our precious children. I will always remember Rhys screaming out hysterically, "Why didn't I die?!" We need to be aware that as parents, we have an obligation to make our surviving multiples feel good about their situations. Only then do I truly believe that our survivors will continue through with a bright and hopeful future.

Joan Woodward sums the situation up perfectly:

> There is a great need to increase the understanding of this unique loss, both among the families and friends of lone twins, as well as among professional carers. The latter seem in general to have shown little awareness of the significance to the survivor of twin loss, which I believe is largely due to ignorance. (Woodward, J., 1998).

It is also an important fact of life that occurrence of loss in multiple pregnancy will sadly, continue. If we aren't prepared to face reality and educate ourselves of the innumerable risks, then I feel that as a society we will continue to set a poor example for generations to come.

For people like myself, Jane Warland, and Julie Bryant, who work hard to promote twin loss issues, I fear that all our efforts will be wasted if we can't do something about improving hospital practice, continue with education programmes on a community level, and show people that it is quite acceptable in a modern society to show tolerance, understanding, sensitivity and love. It amazes me that even after all those years since I had experienced my own loss, very little progress has been made in the area of twin loss and higher order multiple loss care, especially at the hospital stage.

The stories of Australian families disappointed in how their situations were handled; continued. In 2002, with no money and a lot of determination, I approached a small group of Australian and Canadian colleagues and proceeded to put together a collection of information that would hopefully go some way towards filling this void. I had no idea that I would be giving up most of my life for the next four years in order to try and make a difference.

This 'collection', which became known as the "APEX Australia Twin Loss Awareness Kit", went on to win the 2003 South Australian Premier's Community Service Encouragement Award, as well as the 2004 Apex National Donald McKay Citizenship Initiative Award the following year. It was also accepted as the 2005/2006 Apex National

Service Project, and was noted on the Apex Australia website as being one of their most successful.

Whilst waiting for APEX to decide about taking the project onto the next level, that is, nationally, the concept was almost stolen right from under us by another multiple birth support group, to whom we had generously donated several of the earlier South Australian kits. This particular group, who were caught out by our Canadian colleagues for being dishonest, thought they could gain from all our hard work by making their own copy-cat version of the kit. The plan was then to donate these copy-cat versions to the same hospitals to which we were already planning to distribute. However, after much heated online discussion, we successfully argued our case; changing their minds before they were able to 'gazump' us.

Interestingly enough, when I have mentioned these kits to health care professionals who work in some of the hospitals where donations were made, they have not known anything about them. It is therefore my personal opinion that the problem in donating resource materials to places such as hospitals is that after a while they either disappear out the door with someone who doesn't bother to return them, or they lay dormant in some back cupboard until they are thrown away. Either way, it displays a dreadful waste of valuable resource material.

However, back in December 2002, both Jane Warland and I were fortunate in being invited to attend a meeting in Adelaide held by the South Australian/Northern Territory State Board of the APEX club, to present our case for the proposed funding of this unique project. Here is the speech that I presented to the State Board members, explaining the reasons for the kit, what each kit would contain and to whom they were aimed. I truly believed that these kits would help to build that positive future that I have already spoken of, for both the surviving twins and their immediate families.

Hopefully, this project did have a positive, flow-on effect somewhere out in the wider community that changed someone's life for the better. I would like to think so. The phone call I received many years ago during breakfast, from an Adelaide Grandmother thanking me for creating the kit project, and for writing "The Diary", left me with that little glimmer of hope that I may have actually succeeded in helping at least one person to better understand the trials of twin loss.

Speech to Apex South Australian State Board, December 2002.

As far back as the 1980's medical authorities acknowledged that twin pregnancies occurred naturally in approximately one in ninety pregnancies amongst European women, and to a lesser degree amongst women from other cultural backgrounds. However, the increased reliance upon IVF (In Vitro Fertilization) treatment and fertility drugs has seen a dramatic increase in multiple pregnancies with a chance of one in five resulting from IVF, and one in ten resulting from fertility drug use.

Twin pregnancy has long been acknowledged by obstetricians as posing an increased risk to both mother and babies, and often women are admitted to hospital at some stage during the pregnancy for a compulsory rest. Often though, in spite of careful management by medical staff, things go wrong and it is at this point where medical professionals may begin to act badly due to a lack of experience with such cases.

Whilst management of singleton loss has greatly improved over the past decade, there has not been the same degree of advancement in management of loss in multiple pregnancy cases. This holds especially true when one baby lives and the other one dies. Many times, the baby who dies is not acknowledged by medical staff, who in their attempts to comfort the family and avoid causing further pain, encourage the bereaved parents to be glad that they still have a living baby.

However, this well-meaning attempt to focus on the positive side of life, doesn't allow for the need of there parents to also grieve the loss of the deceased child, and unresolved issues regarding this grief may remain for years. Families who raise a surviving twin or higher order multiple speak of having to live with a constant daily reminder of their loss. Survivors often speak of feeling isolated form the rest of the world; trying to understand why they feel 'different'.

Families who suffer multiple pregnancy loss are not always offered the options of 'memory creation' and leave from work as their singleton loss counterparts often are. These families may become fearful to openly grieve for their loss, or losses, and may even resort to refusing to acknowledge the unique situation of the surviving twin by not talking about the child who has died, openly at home. This only adds to the emotional turmoil of the survivors as they too struggle to cope with their own feelings of loss, even loss that has occurred at birth, which is recognised by overseas authorities as being one of the most significant forms.

Therefore, there arises a great need for medical professionals to be better informed in areas relating to multiple pregnancy loss from a parental point of view. It is good to see stories in the media that the medical profession has begun to acknowledge the need to improve doctor/patient communications, and 'bed-side manner' in areas relating to cancer patients, so it is hoped that this communications path may one day extend to families who suffer multiple pregnancy loss.

The 'Australian Twin Loss Awareness Kit' is a unique project, inspired by an overseas model, and is mostly aimed at catering for the needs of Australian families who lose a baby in a multiple pregnancy, but are still faced with the daunting task of raising a survivor. It is a project that aims to place 500 kits containing information and books relating to best practice for medical professionals, including midwives, into hospitals around Australia.

The eventual goal is to provide better care for families at the hospital stage. Most available information is not

'Australian specific' and it is important for Australian families, and the professionals who care for them, to know that there are organisations in this country that cater for twin loss and higher order loss issues.

By families being treated with care and respect, and properly informed about their needs and rights, it is hoped that the long-term effects of loss in such circumstances will be less traumatic. If APEX is prepared to undertake this project, I am sure that these surviving twins and higher order multiples will have a positive future; medical professionals will feel that they have made a worthwhile contribution in this particular area of bereavement care, and APEX will have made another impressive impact upon the Australian community.

Each kit contains the following items:

- **2 brochures – Australian Twin to Twin Transfusion Syndrome Support Group**. One brochure is aimed at medical professionals, and the other is aimed at parents. It provides information about Twin-to-Twin Transfusion Syndrome, and gives suggestions as to best practice and care for families.

- **3 booklets - OzMOST** (Aussie Mums Of Surviving Twins). Two copies of the brochure aimed at parents will be included, along with one copy of the brochure aimed at medical professionals. These brochures list suggestions on how to care for families who suffer twin loss, the encouragement of memory creation, recognizing the twin who has died, as well as the survivor, and provides a recommended reading list and valuable contact groups who can provide further care, information and emotional support. This information has been collated by actual parents of surviving twins who felt that their needs could have been better met during their times of loss.

- **2 copies of the book, "The Diary"** by author Lynne Schulz. This book, (which is already being utilized around the world by bereaved families, other bereavement care organisations as well as some medical professionals), tells the story of a woman who has experienced twin loss, and the reactions of friends, family as well as medical staff as they struggled with very little, if any, knowledge of how to handle such a situation. This book was utilized as a reference in Jane Warland's textbook for midwives.

- **1 copy of the book, "The Midwife and the Bereaved Family"** by Adelaide midwife/author Jane Warland. This is a textbook that devotes a whole chapter to suggested care for families experiencing twin and higher order multiple loss. It has become a valuable tool in the education of medical professionals.

(Schulz, L., 2002)

As a result of our speech, Apex members voted in favour of the idea at their next annual state convention. The kit project was then accepted and trialed on a state level, with the Apex State Board funding the purchase of the kit componentry, and the Apex members providing the labour.

Having joined as a member of Apex, I was able to directly work in conjunction with The Apex Club of Murray Bridge, becoming the project's coordinator, and overseeing all facets of production, including publicity, ordering of componentry, collation of kits, filling orders and distribution. Twin Loss Kits were donated to sixty-six maternity hospitals around South Australia and the Northern Territory during 2003. The award we won later that year provided enough money to fund an extra seventy kits, donated to emergency service groups, church groups, schools, as well as other bereavement care charities throughout the wider community.

I hope that this book, "The Survivor" will follow on from "The Diary", in helping to fill the void that many twin loss families have experienced over the years in obtaining useful and accurate information. I would like to think it could also prove a positive starting point or 'ice-breaker' by showing both medical professionals and parents the benefits of working together.

> *"Live as if you were to die tomorrow. Learn as if you were to live forever".*
>
> *(Mahatma Gandhi).*

Memory Triggers

"Major events in any child's life, such as beginning kindergarten, or starting primary or high school should be associated with feelings of happiness and joy. However, for families with surviving twins, and other higher order multiples, these events can cruelly remind them of that 'missing' part of the twin/triplet/quadruplet picture, i.e. the twin/triplet/quadruplet who has died."

(Used with permission from the NTLS brochure 'Surviving Twins')

REFERENCES

> **Note:** Website addresses shown under 'References' and 'Further Reading' were accurate at the time of accessing the material used in this publication, and have therefore been retained in this listing. Please be advised that over time, these sites may have been removed, or may have changed internet provider addresses. Use of a reliable search engine will no doubt, prove useful in locating them.

American Family Physician, Dec. 1998, Letters to the Editor, Dealing with Loss in Multiple Pregnancies, <http://www.aafp.org/afp/981200ap/letters.html>

Bryant, J., 2002, Jules' story about her twins, Thomas & Megan, <http://www.lm.net.au/~schulz/siss/Julesstory.htm>

Bulow, L., 2002, The twins Eva and Miriam Mozes survived Auschwitz, <http://www.auschwitz.dk/eva.htm>

Fritz, M.A., University of North Carolina, 2000, Hospital Practice, Addressing the Dramatic Rise in Multiple Pregnancies, The McGraw-Hill Companies,

<http://www.hosppract.com/issues/2000/04/fritz.htm?3b0bvr781c>

Funk & Wagnalls New Encyclopedia, 1973, GANNE-GREEK, Vol. 11, Funk & Wagnalls Inc., United States.

Harford, L., Nov 2013, National Twin Loss Support Newsletter, November 2013 Edition, *Multiple Birth Loss Statistics,* p.2.

Hunt, S., May 1997, Potential Connections Between Female Monozygotic Twinning and X-chromosome Inactivation, <http://www.sccs.swarthmore.edu/users/99/shunt/embryo.html>

Jones, D., M.D., Assistant Professor, Dept Obstetrics and Gynecology, Division of Maternal and Fetal Medicine, Yale University School of Medicine, date unknown, Loss and Multi-fetal pregnancies, Vol.2 No.8, <http://www.hygeia.org/poems20.htm>

Leonard, L. G., RN, MSN, Oct. 2001, Prenatal Behaviour of Multiples: Implications for Families and Nurses, AWHONN, the Association of Women's Health, Obstetric and Neonatal Nurses, <http://jognn.awhonn.org/cgi/content/full/31/3/248>

Ndi, R., 2000, The Material Culture of Twins in West Africa, <http://www.sfu.ca/archaeology/museum/ndi/index.html>

Pector, E. A., M.D., Aug. 2002, Rebuilding Life After Loss in Multiple Birth, paper,

<http://www.synspectrum.com/articles.html>

Pector, E. A., M.D., Jun. 2002, Twin Death and Mourning Worldwide: a review of the literature, Twin Res 2002 Jun;5(3):196-205, abstract.

Pector, E. A., M.D., Jan. 2001, Raising survivors of multiple birth loss: What can parents expect?

<http://www.synspectrum.com/articles.html>

Schulz, L, Dec. 2002, Speeches and Papers, Talk Given to APEX South Australia State Board Meeting, Saturday 14th December 2002, West Beach, South Australia, The 'Australian Twin Loss Awareness Kit',

<http://www.lm.net.au/~schulz/siss/share.htm>

Schulz, L., Dec. 1998, The Diary, p.10, 43, 49-50, 52-53, 57-58, 72, 78, 79, 81, Clever-Clogs Independent Publishers, Adelaide

Twin Majority, 2002, Humans are evolving to have twins, <http://195.147.246.213/~twinmajority/>

Ulrich, G., 1996, Yoruba Twin Figure Carvings – Thunderchildren: Yoruba Twin Figure Carvings from Nigeria, <http://www.mpm.edu/collect/yoruba.html>

Warland, J., Jul. 2000, The Midwife and the Bereaved Family, p.89, 97, 100-101, 138, 139, Ausmed Publications Melbourne

Warland, J., 1996, Pregnancy After Loss, with Michael Warland, p. 107, 108, 109, J&M Warland, Adelaide

Woodward, J., 1999, The Lone Twin, A Study in Bereavement and Loss, p. 3-5, 17, 35, 155-156, Free Association Books, London

FURTHER READING

Bickley, C., Mar. 2001, Toronto Sun, 'Saved' by a monster, Film documents Mengele horror, <http://www.canoe.ca/TelevisionShowsL/leosjourney.html>

Blackwell, D., date unknown, *The Worlds Fastest Indian, The Munro Special,* < http://web.archive.org/web/20110723101934/http://www.indianmotorbikes.com/features/munro/munro.htm>. [Accessed 12 Apr 2014]

Fritz, M.A., University of North Carolina, 2000, Hospital Practice, Addressing the Dramatic Rise in Multiple Pregnancies, The McGraw-Hill Companies, <http://www.hosppract.com/issues/2000/04/fritz.htm?3b0bvr781c>

Hayton, A., 2007, Edited, Untwinned: perspectives on the death of a twin before birth, Wren Publications, St Albans, England

Li Z, Zeki, R, Hilder, L & Sullivan, E.A., 2012, *Australia's mothers and babies 2010,* Perinatal statistics series no 27. Cat.

No. PER 57. Canberra: AIHW National Perinatal Epidemiology and Statistics Unit

Mani, the Ambassador of Ligh, date unknown, His Life and Times, <http://www.mystae.com/restricted/streams/gnosis/mani.html>

Metro Plus Bangalore, Jul. 2002, The Hindu, Seeing Double, <http://www.hinduonnet.com/thehindu/mp/2002/07/11/stories/2002071100420100.htm>

Pector, E. A., M.D., Jun. 2002, Twin death and mourning worldwide: a review of the literature. Twin Res 2002 Jun;5(3):196-205, paper. Contact E.A. Pector: Pector@enteract.com.

Schulz, L., June 2002, National Twin Loss Support website, <http://www.nationaltwinloss.org.au>

Twain and Twins, date unknown, <http://etext.lib.virginia.edu/railton/wilson/mttwins.html>

GLOSSARY

APEX – Australian Community Service Club. Refer website <http://www.apex.org.au/>

Banshee – fairy or other form of supernatural being. Often associated with horror and known for emitting loud screams.

Bereavement counsellor – person who guides, helps or enlightens another person after someone has died.

Brekky – Australian slang term for 'breakfast'.

Cerebral Palsy – intellectual paralysis where the nerves sending the messages from the brain to the muscles do not function in a coordinated manner.

Conjoined twins – (formerly referred to as 'Siamese twins'); twins who are physically joined together at some part of their bodies.

Cuppa – Common Australian slang term for 'cup of tea or coffee'.

Endorphin – a naturally produced protein within the body that sends messages to the brain to diminish pain, and thus results in a sedative-like effect on the body.

Ethical – moral principles

Fine Motor Skills – the coordination of the various body parts for subtle work, for example, using the thumb and forefinger to pick something up and includes writing and drawing skills.

Gestation – the period of time that a baby is carried in the womb.

Gazump – a term usually associated with the buying and selling of real estate, but also used as a slang term for the unethical practice of getting in before someone else, even though two parties may have already made a verbal agreement regarding a matter. Regarded as 'playing unfair'.

Gnostic – a person who follows 'Gnosticism', *i.e. the term applied to several religious philosophies, both Christian and pagan, that stressed the revelation of mystical knowledge as the key to salvation. (Funk & Wagnalls, 1973).*

Gross Motor Skills – the ability of a person to control different parts of their body for large movement, for example walking, running.

Harbinger – forerunner, omen, prediction, an evil omen.

Ice-breaker – an action or words used when addressing a group of people to make the audience, or group participants to feel more comfortable and at ease with each other. A useful communication tool for the introduction of strangers.

Instinctive behaviours – patterns of behaviour that are influenced by hereditary characteristics, and environmental effects.

IVF – In Vitro Fertilization; a reproductive technology involving the removal of a female egg and a male sperm, and creating the fertilization process outside the body in a flat dish.

Memory creation – collecting physical items that will assist a person to remember someone who has died. Commonly utilized in infant death situations.

Monochorionic – one placenta, identical twins.

Neonatal death – death within a few hours, days or weeks after birth.

Neurological – medical definition relating to nervous bodily functioning.

NICU – Neonatal Intensive Care Unit.

Primary socialisation – the basic learning skills gained during early childhood, usually from within the family unit.

Secondary socialisation – the impressions gained during middle to late childhood, mostly from within the school environment, but also from religious practices and the mass media.

Singleton – one baby in the womb, i.e. not a multiple pregnancy.

Stillbirth – (Australian definition) baby born after 20 weeks gestation of at least 400g showing no signs of life at birth. (UK definition - after 24 weeks, USA definition – after 27 weeks).

Tenet – any opinion, principle or doctrine regarded as being true.

Ultrasound – High frequency sound waves used to diagnose various conditions within the body. Also referred to as a 'sonogram'.

Vex – to annoy, puzzle or confuse.

USEFUL ORGANISATIONS

(Internet)

If you look closely and spend a bit of time 'surfing' or exploring the Internet, you will find many useful organisations that provide interesting information regarding twin loss issues. However, it takes a great deal more time and patience to discover and learn which sites are going to be of good use. Here are a few useful key words that will definitely assist in finding the groups listed further in this chapter:

- twin loss
- special needs children
- surviving twins
- lone twin
- womb-mate
- womb twin survivor
- TTTS
- Twinless twins
- CLIMB
- Twins
- Lynne Schulz
- Lynne Harford

- Lynda P Haddon
- Elizabeth Pector

A more comprehensive and up-to-date list of support groups can be found on the National Twin Loss Support website at <http://www.nationatwinloss.org.au>. Each group in turn provides their own list of support organisations and bereavement care resources.

Survivor Guilt

"We must be aware that surviving multiple birth children suffer guilt of being just that - a survivor. They experience emotions similar to those experienced by war veterans, accident victims, and people who have endure major natural disasters. Psychological studies done over the years support this."

(Used with permission from the NTLS brochure 'Don't give up Hope!')

APPENDIX I

NATIONAL TWIN LOSS SUPPORT

Based in Adelaide, South Australia, National Twin Loss Support (NTLS) continues to make an impact in Australia and overseas. After celebrating its 21st Anniversary in October 2013, this small, independently operated organisation continues to specialise in providing information to health care professionals, multiple birth loss families, as well as other bereavement care organisations free of charge. The Founder has moved away from personal counselling to focus on writing original material for use in newsletters, brochures and books. Whilst the website still provides avenues through which interested persons may obtain twin loss information, find links to other organisations, and seek support, the Facebook page continues to increase in popularity.

NTLS began in October 1992 in Murray Bridge, South Australia, under the name of "The Murraylands Lutheran Stillborn Infant Support Service". Its aim was to bridge the gap between rural and city facilities in the area of infant loss. However, changes in modern technology have inevitably changed the way the world communicates. Most homes now have internet access and most people own a mobile phone. NTLS has become an important player in providing information relating to twin loss issues right around the world.

Due to the competitive nature of the bereavement care industry as a whole, counselling services are no longer offered. The NTLS website provides links to numerous professional counselling bodies in countries such as Australia, the United States, the United Kingdom, Canada and New Zealand. The objective is not to replicate resources, (which is regarded as time wasting and confusing for those seeking assistance), but to network in with existing facilities. This is what made NTLS unique in the first place; the fact that the founder wanted to work with other groups, instead of duplicating what was already in existence. For example, NTLS attempts to produce original material in its quarterly newsletters, whilst many other bereavement care groups reproduce articles obtained from the same sources, on a repetitive basis.

NTLS Founder, Lynne Harford is not only the mother of a Surviving Twin, but a trained bereavement counsellor; having completed government accredited counselling courses through Lutheran Community Care in Adelaide, and a Grief Counselling course through the Bonnie Babes Foundation Inc., Victoria. To improve her knowledge and skills, Lynne even completed the Graduate Certificate in Counselling Skills through the Australian College of Applied Psychology in 2012.

In 2003, Australian statistics revealed that up to one in three pregnancies resulted in miscarriage, stillbirth, or neo-natal death, (i.e. death shortly after birth). Whilst statistics pertaining directly to twin and higher order multiple birth loss remain relatively scarce when compared to singleton loss statistics, in 2012 the Australian Institute of Health and Welfare, in Canberra Australia, published in its annual findings that:

...the neonatal death rate of twins was 17.6 per 1,000 live births and 58.1 per 1,000 births in higher order multiple pregnancies. Their conclusion was that multiple birth loss was greater than singleton loss (2.4 per 1,000 live births). (Harford, L., Nov. 2013)

The book, "The Diary", which is the prequel to "The Survivor", has become a valuable extension of the work done by National Twin Loss Support, and continues to be utilised by many different organisations within the wider community. "The Diary" was utilized as a reference in Jane Warland's textbook for midwives entitled, "The Midwife and the Bereaved Family". It was also promoted by the Multiple Birth Foundation in London in early 2000, at their annual bereavement day.

Over the years, National Twin Loss Support has supported other bereavement care organisations, as well as community based groups. It has donated books about loss and grief to bereavement care to local schools, hospitals, libraries and women's information centres to assist the general community with bereavement care education and awareness. For several years it found success with Internet counselling, due to its determined stand on promoting multiple pregnancy loss issues.

During 2002 to 2006, with the blessing of the Canadian Multiple Birth Group, NTLS initiated a partnership with Apex Australia, and produced the Apex Australia Twin Loss Awareness Kit. Kits were donated to all maternity hospitals in South Australia and the Northern Territory. The kit was the winner of the 2003 South Australian Premier's Community Service Encouragement Award. With the assistance of Apex clubs around Australia, the Apex Australia Twin Loss Awareness Kit was donated to community service organisations, church groups, schools and medical centres, and went on to become one of Apex's most successful projects

Since that time, numerous other infant loss organisations have attempted to replicate the feat through the production of their own kits. However, NTLS prides itself on being one of the first to produce a truly Australian-specific product, which promoted the work of Australian bereavement care authors such as Jane Warland and Lynne Schulz.

National Twin Loss Support is registered as a Deductible Gift Recipient by the Australian Taxation Office. (ABN: 69 695 149 922).

> **Being open and honest**
>
> "So much has been written about the negative impact upon surviving multiple birth children, especially those who experience their loss early in life. However, by being open and honest about your survivor's situation, their ability to cope, and accept, is strongly enhanced."
>
> *(Used with permission from the NTLS brochure 'Don't give up Hope!')*

APPENDIX II

EXPERT LIST

- **John Bowlby:** (1907-1990). British Psychoanalyst and Psychiatrist. Although initially respected during the earlier stages of his career by his peers, he eventually became considered as extremely controversial in his thinking, particularly with his ideas pertaining to twin loss grief. Known for his ideas regarding 'Attachment Theory'.

- **Julie Bryant:** Former Grief Counsellor based in NSW, Australia. Founder of OzMOST (Aussie Mums Of Surviving Twins). Julie is also a mother of a surviving twin.

- **Lynda P. Haddon:** Canadian Multiple Birth Educator and Past President of the Multiple Births Families Association in Ottawa, and the Multiple Births group in Canada. Author of much support literature for families of multiples. Lynda has three adult daughters; Shayna, and twins, Holly and Emily.

- **Rachel Ndi:** West African archaeologist, who specialises in the area of 'ethnoarchaeology', i.e. the study of living societies. Rachel is a mother of twins.

- **Elizabeth A Pector:** American family physician based in Naperville, Illinois. Author of many articles and papers regarding twin loss issues. Elizabeth is the mother of a surviving twin.

- **Alessandra Piontelli:** Visiting Professor of Child Neuropsychiatry, University of Milan, Italy. Author of the book, "Twins: From Fetus to Child".

- **Jane Warland:** Australian Senior University Lecturer and former midwife, based in Adelaide, South Australia. Author of the books "Our Baby Died", "Pregnancy After Loss" and "The Midwife and the Bereaved Family". Jane is also a bereaved parent who has suffered both a miscarriage and a stillbirth.

- **Joan Woodward:** British psychotherapist based in Birmingham, England. Founder of the Lone Twin Network (LTN), and author of the book, "The Lone

Twin, Understanding Twin Bereavement and Loss".

Joan is a surviving twin.

APPENDIX III

CARE INVESTIGATION

As the years progressed, I remained unconvinced that any major improvements in care had occurred in the area of twin and higher order multiple birth loss. This was due to the fact that people were still contacting me with stories about how they were being treated by health care professionals, as well as family and friends. I felt frustrated that the work done during 2002-2006 had gone mostly unnoticed, and for that reason alone, I felt that I had somehow failed in achieving the goal of initiating change.

I was interested to find out more, so during 2008-2010 I conducted my own investigation into the quality and type of care being provided by health care professionals to multiple birth loss families, particularly after the hospital stay. My initial efforts hit a huge brick wall within the medical profession due to my lack of medical qualifications. Being a twin loss parent, as well as a trained counsellor, who had founded a rather small twin loss organisation, did not hold much credence with many health care professionals.

They were horrified to even consider the notion that a mere 'mother', without any formal medical training, could have anything of value to teach them. They were therefore unwilling to assist in the distribution of the questionnaires to any of their patients. There were also privacy and confidentiality issues to consider as well.

My thoughts however, remained the exact opposite. I felt that since the medical profession had improved its care of patients and families experiencing cancer for example, by listening to the patients and their families, that the same would work for twin and higher order multiple birth loss care. Sounded ideal, but that's where I was wrong. So, like the twin loss kits, if I wanted to learn more, so that I could voice the opinions of those who really needed to be heard, then I would have to find another way.

Running out of ideas about how to actually get started, I sought advice from my good friend, Dr Jane Warland PhD, who provided useful insight into the thinking of those health care professionals whom I was trying to educate. Jane herself had spent several years conducting infant loss research, so she assisted me in the creation of a questionnaire. We decided it was probably going to be more effective contacting multiple birth loss parents via the National Twin Loss Support website, as well as promoting the 'cause' through several other volunteer bereavement care organisations with whom I had established useful contacts.

It did not take long for completed questionnaires to arrive via email and post; not only from within Australia, but to my delight, from countries such as the United States, Canada and New Zealand. All participants were unpaid, ranging in ages from 28 to 48 years. Ten women had lost one twin; four women had lost both, whilst one mother had lost all her three triplets. The years in which their losses actually occurred ranged from 1983 to 2010. Reasons for loss varied. The majority of losses occurred as a result of twin-to-twin transfusion syndrome, one from feotal distress, one from infection, one from SIDS, and the rest of the babies died of unknown causes.

Thank you to the fifteen mothers who took part in the investigation. Although acknowledging that the number of participants in this study is rather small, their responses have proven useful in confirming my fears that not a lot has changed since my own twin loss in early 1990.

The following responses reveal that the care experience, whether positive or negative, can be unpredictable at best. After all the years since my own loss in 1990, the following results still fall into the broad category of "hit and miss". Some families have been well supported by health care professionals, as well as family and friends, whilst others have been very poorly treated indeed.

For multiple birth loss parents reading this, you will no doubt experience some strong memory triggers. Please be gentle on yourselves. For any health care professionals reading this, I hope these experiences force you to examine your actions towards multiple birth loss families. The words from these mothers will either reinforce that you are doing good work in this area; or will challenge you to reconsider your methods if you are not.

Question: Did you feel that your physical and emotional needs were met when you were in hospital?

Joanne – Canada (Aug 2008): *"Yes, in the general hospital in North Bay."*

Elizabeth – Canada (Sep 2008): *"Emotional –no. As a staff member who also delivers babies it was clear the nursing staff didn't know what to do with me. Pastoral support was useless. No follow up post discharge from the hospital or agencies."*

Jane – New Zealand (Apr 2009): *"It was only the kindness of two nurses who took extra special care of me and our situation. One of the midwives is a personal friend and it was her who took the* *initiative to take footprints and photos for us, and give us the literature about the twinloss community. After the manual removal of the placenta and I was coming out of the anesthetic, I was in a recovery room where the lady behind the next curtain was nursing her newborn twins. This was possibly the most confusing and heartbreaking thing I had to deal with.*

I have been assured that the new hospital that has just been built would prevent this happening to anyone else. I doubt that I would have had much support if it hadn't been for our friend 'on the inside'. One ward nurse even came into the room on the day of the delivery and asked me where my baby was and told me to walk around even though she could see I had tubes attached to me."

Kim – Australia (May 2008): *"Unfortunately not at all. I had no support from any medical or professional help during my three months stay, or referrals after. (Although my private doctor was fantastic!)"*

Jenny – Australia (May 2008): *"Not really. I guess the physical care was ok, but not the emotional. Very much the days of, 'lucky you still have another'."*

Question: Did you feel that your physical and practical needs were met during the early weeks, months or years after your loss, for example, help with daily chores, care for other children?

Linda – Australia (Oct 2008): *"I felt that I could get emotional support if I needed it, i.e. from SANDS (Stillborn And Neonatal Death Support), and from my parents."*

Narelle – Australia (Oct 2008): *"We had to relocate to Perth for four months and although the hospital had off-site accommodation for myself; husbands and children couldn't stay. Also we could have applied for money for accommodation but it would not have covered the rents in the area where the hospital is located. I could have applied for an allowance to help with travel costs from Bunbury to Perth but it was only for me, and not my husband. We didn't apply for that as I had to stay in Perth whilst my husband travelled back and forth. Back in Bunbury, I was offered home help from before the twins were born, and over a year later I am still getting some, for example, from the Red Cross, and also South West Emergency Care."*

Emily – USA (May 2008): *"My work did give me three weeks off to recover. I was home with my 3 year old at the time so she kept me busy."*

Sylvia – Australia (May 2009): *"Family and friends were very supportive during this time and assisted with some chores and child minding."*

Sally – Australia (Jun 2008): *"We utilised childcare through the hospital, and as the hospital was a long way from home, we were accommodated in hospital units which was wonderful. When we returned home we were offered three months of free childcare, we were also offered homehelp but I (stupidly!) refused."*

Question: Did you feel that your psychological and emotional needs were met by your healthcare professional?

Rachell – New Zealand (Jan 2009): *"No, I felt that people expected anti-depressants to dull the pain and make it all better ... they didn't."*

Angela – Australia (May 2008): *"No. The hospital advised they would call the family clinic (where I was to get Macy's weight etc., monitored), in advance to advise them of my situation and ask that I receive home visits for a while, and that someone would call me to arrange this. No-one called. I was anxious to have my surviving twin checked on. When I called the clinic myself after 1 week at home, I had to start from scratch and was told that if I wanted a home visit I* *could be waiting for another two to three weeks ...so I had to make my own way to the clinic.*

... still feel they don't really know what services to provide you with. They routinely recommend you to a social worker ... it was just a question and answer session ... that doesn't help you with any coping mechanisms to get through the days."

Bindi – Australia (May 2010): *They confused me, some told me I wasn't coping because of grief, some said depression. They showed me three different ways to express milk, and different advice ... - I felt very confused. Some said sleep if you want to and others said go feed baby."*

Anonymous – Australia (Oct 2008): *"I think the Doctors did the best they could under the circumstances. Their concern was genuine and non-judgmental. After an incident in which I was taken to hospital by ambulance, my Dr suggested I see the visiting psychiatrist, which I did. One Dr also asked how I was coping, on a few occasions outside of his practice, and offered his services free of charge at any time."*

Annette – Australia (May 2008): *"They offered counselling and the midwives were wonderful. The obstetricians were fairly oblivious to my loss, though they saw it as more of a test case as Gosford had* never dealt with anything like that before. I found some of the Registrars to be very abrupt and not willing to assist me with my concerns about the birth and the growth rate of Stephanie."

Question: How did you feel your needs were met, or not met, by your family and/or friends?

Joanne – Canada (Aug 2008): *"One member of a family was supportive. A couple of long distance friends we never met at least sent a card. And one local friend was supportive. We had no support from anyone else. The worst part was that none of our sisters, (both sides of the family), had any interest in the loss of our sons, and only two persons showed up at the funeral."*

Bindi – Australia (May 2010): *"Family hassled me about arranging a funeral the same day I got discharged. Social worker told us home help etc., would come and help, but never did. Friends kept ringing, which was annoying as I couldn't talk properly."*

Angela – Australia (May 2008): *"Some family didn't even contact me, probably because they didn't know what to say, but I found it so bizarre that at a most terrible time in my life, they were completely absent. Some close family members kept asking if I was better, which drove me to despair; I wasn't ill! No-one seemed to know what to do* *for the best, including me. I realise now that I just needed someone to listen to me, someone who wasn't going to get uncomfortable with my grief, and who wasn't going to try and offer solutions; just someone to listen with compassion, was probably what I needed.*

My husband thought by talking about things, and talking about Callum specifically, would result in me taking a back step. I tried to explain a couple of times this was not the case, talking and crying eased the weight I was carrying. A close friend who was with me a lot after I lost Callum, after five months, stopped asking about things, and coming to see me, which has made me feel she thinks I should be over it by now, and I don't feel I can tell her how things are when they get bad. Another close friend has fortunately, been there for me from the start, and is still sensitive towards my loss now, and will ask how I am, and I feel I can tell her truthfully how I feel."

Question: Briefly describe anything that the healthcare professionals did that you considered unhelpful?

Sally – Australia (Jun 2008): *"Booking me into a six week check up at the antenatal ward."*

Annette – Australia (May 2008): *"Most Registrars and Obstetricians I came across only considered it a single pregnancy and treated it as such. They weren't concerned about their [the babies] tangling, as the membrane had been broken, nor her slow growth rate, which was a major concern to me as Steph had been the donor twin. One Obstetrician came in two weeks after my loss without reading my notes and congratulated me on expecting twins."*

Emily – USA (May 2008): *"It took over thirty-six hours in the hospital for me before they were born. There should be some better alternatives besides the 'pill' to make my cervix open up. Everyone who came to visit had to go through the Delivery Unit where everyone was happy and cheerful then to see me."*

Question: Briefly describe some of the things that the health care professionals did for your baby/ies that you considered helpful?

Kim – Australia (May 2008): *"Nothing. I was very let down. It wasn't until years later, talking to OZMOST (Aussie Mums Of Surviving Twins) girls, I learnt things I could have done, e.g. bath her, dress her myself, had contact with her more and take lots of photos."*

Sylvia – Australia (May 2009): *"Referring to the twin who died by their name, even before they were born. Organising counselling – although the counselling didn't really help much, it was nice that they went out of their way to organise it for me. The feotal medicine midwife kept a check on how I was going while I was still in the hospital environment. The doctors made sure I was allowed out of the hospital for a few hours to attend my baby's funeral when I had been re-hospitalised with an infection after the birth."*

Narelle – Australia (Oct 2008): *"During hospital stays (both pre and post birth), listened to me. Call my babies by their names. Say they were sorry. Wash and dress Luke. Visit after the birth just to see how I was doing. Attend Luke's naming service at the hospital. Do hand and footprints, take photos, and save mementos. Help me persist with breastfeeding. Take Joshua when I needed a break. Made sure that everyone who entered my room knew the situation."*

Question: Are you aware of what twin loss resources are available locally, nationally, or internationally?

Rachell – New Zealand (Jan 2009): *"Only by my own research. Doesn't seem to be a lot of information, unless you are actively* *searching. I have, and would help with this now, before anyone else needs to use it."*

Linda – Australia (Oct 2008): *"We have access to SANDS (Stillborn And Neonatal Death Support) libraries, and staff, so feel we have a lot of resources at hand. We also source information from the internet."*

Elizabeth – Canada (Sep 2008): *"Only because I did a LOT of internet research, especially as I returned to work seven months later. I still don't know of any resources for (primary) maternity care providers who suffer loss. It was very hard having my patients who knew I was expecting twins, as I care for them in their pregnancies, return in their later pregnancies and ask, "so how did your birth go and how are your twins?" It's a VERY hard question to take on in the middle of your office day."*

Question: Did you feel comfortable dealing with your health care professional? For example, would you ever go back to them if the need arose?

Jenny – Australia (May 2008): *"Not for anything to do with myself, nothing emotionally, or my grief."*

Jane – New Zealand (Apr 2009): *"No."*

Anonymous – Australia (Oct 2008): *"Yes."*

∼ Other books by the same author∼

The Diary

Made in the USA
Coppell, TX
02 October 2021